AMERICA'S BRITISH CULTURE

Library of Conservative Thought

AMERICA'S BRITISH CULTURE

Russell Kirk

Transaction Publishers
New Brunswick (U.S.A.) and London (U.K.)

First paperback printing 2005

Copyright © 1993 by Transaction Publishers, New Brunswick, New Jersey.

This book is printed on acid-free paper that meets the American National Standard for Permanence of Paper for Printed Library Materials.

Library of Congress Catalog Number: 92-13217
ISBN: 1-56000-066-X (cloth); 1-4128-0457-4 (paper)
Printed in the United States of America

Library of Congress Cataloging-in-Publication Data

Kirk, Russell.
America's British culture / Russell Kirk.
p. cm.— (The Library of conservative thought)
Includes index.
ISBN 1-4128-0457-4
1. United States—Civilization—British influences. I. Title. II. Series.

E169.1.K549   1992   92-13217
306'.0973—dc20   CIP

To Henry Salvatori,
friend and benefactor for three decades

Contents

Acknowledgments

The author thanks Pepperdine University for sponsoring the writing of this book, and Mr. Henry Salvatori for conceiving of such a study and making it possible. In his library at the Michigan village of Mecosta, the author had the help of several Fellows of the Marguerite Eyer Wilbur Foundation: Miss Kristen Sifert, Miss Amy Verkest, Mr. Matthew Davis, Mr. Earl Ryan, and Mr. William Fahey.

1

The Necessity for a General Culture

What Does "Culture" Mean?

This slim book is a summary account of the culture that the people of the United States have inherited from Britain. Sometimes this is called the Anglo-Saxon culture—although it is not simply English, for much in British culture has had its origins in Scotland, Ireland, and Wales. So dominant has British culture been in America, north of the Rio Grande, from the seventeenth century to the present, that if somehow the British elements could be eliminated from all the cultural patterns of the United States—why, Americans would be left with no coherent culture in public or in private life.

When we employ this word *culture*, what do we signify by it? Does "culture" mean refinement and learning, urbanity and good taste? Or does this "culture" mean the folkways of a people? Nowadays the word may be employed in either of the above significations; nor are these different meanings necessarily opposed one to the other.

Our English word *culture* is derived from the Latin word *cultus*, which to the Romans signified both tilling the soil and worshipping the divine. In the beginning, culture arises from the cult: that is, people are joined together in worship, and out of their religious association grows the organized human community. Common cultivation of crops, common defense, common laws, cooperation in much else—these are the rudiments of a people's culture. If that culture succeeds, it may grow into a civilization.

During the past half-century, such eminent historians as Christopher Dawson, Eric Voegelin, and Arnold Toynbee have described the close connections between religion and culture. As Dawson put it in his Gifford Lectures of 1947,

1

A social culture is an organized way of life which is based on a common tradition and conditioned by a common environment. . . . It is clear that a common way of life involves a common view of life, common standards of behavior and common standards of value, and consequently a culture is a spiritual community which owes its unity to common beliefs and common ways of thought far more than to any unanimity of physical type. . . . Therefore from the beginning the social way of life which is culture has been deliberately ordered and directed in accordance with the higher laws of life which are religion.[1]

Dawson gives us here a quasi-anthropological definition of culture. At the beginning of the twentieth century, historians and men of letters would have raised their eyebrows at this sociological approach. The principal dictionaries of nine decades ago offered diverse definitions of the word—the agricultural meaning, the biological one, the bacteriological one, and others; but the common apprehension of *culture* ran much like this: "The result of mental cultivation, or the state of being cultivated; refinement or enlightenment; learning and taste; in a broad sense, civilization, as, a man of *culture*."

This latter employment of the word, connoting personal achievement of high standards in manners, taste, and knowledge, conjuring up the image of the virtuoso, is not archaic today. But the prevailing anthropological understanding of the word signifies the many elements which a people develop in common. We may take as a working anthropological definition that offered by H. J. Rose, in a footnote to his *Handbook of Latin Literature* (1936).

"By 'culture' is meant simply a mode of communal life characteristically human, i.e., beyond the capacity of any beast," Rose writes. "Refinement and civilization are not implied, although not excluded. Thus we may speak alike of the 'culture' of the Australian blacks and of the modern French, distinguishing them as lower and higher respectively."[2]

To apprehend the relationships between "culture" as the word is employed by anthropologists and "culture" as that word is understood by the champions of high achievements in mind and art, we may turn to the chief poet of this century, T. S. Eliot. Since fairly early in the nineteenth century, reflective men and women have tended to regard this latter sort of culture as something to be sought after. Just what is it that the champions of culture seek? Why, "improvement of the human mind and spirit."[3]

Eliot suggests that this high culture consists of a mingling of manners, aesthetic attainment, and intellectual attainment. He argues too that we should regard culture in three senses, that is, whether we have in mind the development of an individual, or the development of a group or class, or the development of a whole society.

As Eliot explains, the different types of culture are interdependent. The question is not really one of conflict between "democratic" and "aristocratic" modes of culture. A nation's culture may be diverse, seemingly; yet the personal culture cannot long survive if cut off from the culture of a group or class. Nor may the high culture of a class endure if the popular culture is debased, or if the popular culture is at odds with personal and class cultures.

"Cultural disintegration is present when two or more strata so separate that these become in effect distinct cultures, and also when culture at the upper group level breaks into fragments each of which represents one cultural activity alone," Eliot writes. "If I am not mistaken, some disintegration of the classes in which culture is, or should be, most highly developed, has already taken place in western society—as well as some cultural separation between one level of society and another. Religious thought and practice, philosophy and art, all tend to become isolated areas cultivated by groups in no communication with each other."[4]

With increased speed, that lamentable process of disintegration and separation has continued since Eliot wrote those sentences four decades ago; it is especially conspicuous in American higher education. If the decay goes far enough, in the long run a society's culture sinks to a low level; or the society may fall apart altogether. We Americans live, near the end of the twentieth century, in an era when the general outlines and institutions of our inherited culture still are recognizable; yet it does not follow that our children or our grandchildren, in the twenty-first century, will retain a great part of that old culture.

To resume T. S. Eliot's argument, any healthy culture is represented at its higher levels by a class or body of persons of remarkable intelligence and taste, leaders in mind and conscience. Often such persons inherit their positions as guardians of culture; to borrow a phrase from Edmund Burke, these are the men and women who have been reared in "the unbought grace of life."

Either within such a cultured class, or sometimes temporarily outside it, there should be found individuals of cultural attainments whose private talents may contribute much to the improvement of the human mind and spirit. Yet such persons cannot be expected to sustain culture on their own shoulders somehow. Atlas-like, if they lack the support of a class or group, or if the tendency of the great mass of people is in an opposite direction. As Eliot puts it, "People are always ready to consider themselves persons of culture, on the strengths of one proficiency, when they are not only lacking in others, but blind to those they lack."[5]

Beyond the men and women of personal culture, beyond the high culture of class or group, lies the democratic culture of the folk—if we are to speak, like anthropologists, of cultural folkways. The popular culture ordinarily has had its origins, perhaps long ago, in the concepts and customs of a cultural aristocracy, much as the Children of Israel received their culture from Moses and Aaron. And yet once cultural beliefs, traits, conventions, and institutions have taken hold among a people, the most ardent and able adherents and defenders of an inherited culture may be obscure men and women, members of the democratic culture, who maintain the good old cause.

But if the mass culture, the democratic culture, becomes much alienated from the culture of the educated classes—why, presently the mass culture falls into decadence. That has been happening swiftly in recent decades, in America and elsewhere. Thomas Molnar, in his recent book *Twin Powers*, describes the consequences:

> *Culture* has come to mean, of course, anything that happens to catch the fancy of a group: rock concerts, supposedly for the famished of the third world; the drug culture and other subcultures; sects and cults; sexual excess and aberration; blasphemy on stage and screen; frightening and obscene shapes; the plastic wrapping of the Pont-Neuf or the California coast; to smashing of the family and other institutions; the display of the queer, abject, the sick. These instant products, meant to provide instant satisfaction to a society itself unmoored from foundation and tradition, accordingly deny the work of mediation and maturation and favor the incoherent, the shapeless and the repulsive.[6]

Dr. Molnar adds that if this sort of culture "spreads out in moviehouse, museum, festival, press, and university, the reason may be that it embodies society's ideal." Here Molnar is writing of what commonly is called the counterculture—an anticulture which may extend to the very people who are supposed to set high cultural standards. This revolt against inherited culture often hardens into a detestation of those classes and groups, and their standards, which once upon a time shaped the thought and the taste of the whole society. Eliot touches upon this ideological hostility toward any sort of superior culture.

"It is commonly assumed," Eliot puts it, "that there is culture, but that it is the property of a small section of society; and from this assumption it is usual to proceed to one of two conclusions: either that culture can only be the concern of a small minority, and that therefore there is no place for it in the society of the future; or that in the society of the future the culture which has been the possession of the few must be put at the disposal of everybody."[7]

The preferences, mores, and customs that make up the democratic culture used to find their sanction in the judgment of individuals of remarkable talents, or in the manners and attitudes of a class or group of arbiters of culture. For instance, if Chaucer still is taught in some degree in America's public schools, that is not because the Common Teacher or the Common Pupil instinctively recognizes Chaucer's merits; rather, it is because, a good while ago, the people who make up school curricula and publish school textbooks decided that Chaucer ought to be studied, being a great author of historical importance; and so Chaucer has lingered on, as of "cultural value," despite large changes in the schools. If directors of curricula and publishers of textbooks should decide tomorrow to delete Geoffrey Chaucer, the democratic culture of the Representative Parent would not restore poor Chaucer; indeed, the Representative Parent might sigh with relief at the expulsion of the funny old fellow who couldn't write real English.

The culture of the crowd, then, is dependent in the long run upon the culture of the man of genius and the culture of the educated classes. It is equally true that the cultured individual and the cultured class cannot prevail—indeed, cannot survive—if a great wall of separation should be erected between them and the mass of people. What happens to a talented musicologist, say, when ninety-five percent of the rising generation have been subjected in their formative years to acid rock, and have paid no attention whatsoever to the music of elevation and order? What happens to the class of professors of literature, say, when the accustomed reading of most of their male students has been *Playboy* and *Penthouse*?

A received culture may be betrayed by the talented individual or the culturally schooled class of men and women, quite as fatally as by the crowd. A musicologist who casts aside the great composers of the eighteenth and nineteenth centuries out of his enthusiasm for electronic dissonance; a professor of humane letters who lectures obsessively on the perverse in literature—such persons are false to their duty of upholding certain norms of culture. And any hungry sheep of the democratic culture who happen to look up at these mentors—why, if they are fed, it is upon the inedible or the putrescent.

It will not suffice for us who enjoy the old received culture to seek refuge in the embrace of Common, or Popular, Culture. For the Common Culture commonly decides to do tomorrow what the Uncommon Culture does today; or, worse, the Common Culture, bewildered, converts itself into the Common Counterculture. The defense of inherited culture must be conducted here and now, with what weapons may be snatched from the walls—here on this darkling plain at the end of the twentieth century. With Eliot, we conduct

> *. . . a raid on the inarticulate*
> *With shabby equipment always deteriorating . . .*

A nation's traditional culture can endure only if the several elements that compose it admit an underlying unity or fidelity to a common cause. The high culture and the common culture, of necessity, are interdependent; so are the national culture and the regional culture. What American culture urgently requires just now is solidarity: that is, a common front against the operations of Chaos and old Night.

The Enemies of Inherited Culture

"Down with Euroculture!" During the past several years, strident voices have been crying that commination in many states of the Union. The adversaries of the dominant culture in the United States demand that in American schooling, and in American life generally, Eurocentric assumptions must be supplanted by a "multiculture" emphasizing the cultural achievements of "African Americans, Asian Americans, Puerto Ricans/Latinos, and Native Americans." (This list of "minorities" is found in an official report of a task force appointed by the educational commissioner of the State of New York.) The culture of women also is incorporated in some demands for a cultural revolution in America—despite the fact that America's dominant higher culture already, in considerable part, is sustained by intelligent and conscientious women.

Of course it is true that into the culture, the British culture, of North America have entered large elements, in the nineteenth and twentieth centuries, of other major cultures, chiefly from Europe—but also, and increasingly, from China, Japan, the Levant, Mexico, Puerto Rico, and (quite recently) Korea and Indochina. But these and other cultures from abroad have been peacefully incorporated into the dominant British culture of North America. Even Mexican culture, which soon may be the biggest minority ethnic bloc in the United States, commonly is woven into the fabric of American society—after the passage of a single generation.

Now American society is imperfect, as is everything else here below. Yet the transplanted culture of Britain in America has been one of humankind's more successful achievements. The United States today is flooded with immigrants, lawful or unlawful, eager to enjoy the security, prosperity, freedom, and cultural opportunities of America. America's successes, substantially, have been made possible by the vigor of the British culture that most Americans now take for granted. Who, then, are the people desiring to pull down this dominant culture and set up in its place some amorphous "multiculture"?

One does not find the Vietnamese, or other Asiatics who have taken refuge in America, complaining about "cultural oppression." Most of them swiftly and intelligently adapt themselves to American culture. Most Spanish-surname Americans do not deny the merits of European civilization. Of "Native Americans," only a handful pretend to desire some sort of return to their ancestors' folkways of the eighteenth century. One hears no cultural howls of rage from Eskimo or Aleut.

In truth, the adversaries of America's dominant culture may be classified in three categories: certain militant blacks; white radicals, mostly "civil rights" zealots of yesteryear; and a mob of bored, indolent students to whom any culture but pop culture is anathema. Near the close of the twentieth century, the hardest haters of inherited high culture are to be found within the Academy—embittered ideologues, their character warped in the turbulent 'sixties, whose ambition it is to pull down whatever has long been regarded as true and noble. On nearly every campus, some of the purported guardians of culture have become the destroyers of culture. Ratlike, they gnaw at the foundations of society—quite as Karl Marx admonished intellectuals to do. At bottom, this "Down with Euroculture!" is the symptom of an intellectual disease that has been festering for a quarter of a century and longer.

The malign silliness of the academic radicals' shrieks is sufficiently suggested by their complaint that most books prescribed for college reading, were written by "dead white males"—as if one might alter retroactively the pigmentation and the gender of William Shakespeare or Isaac Newton. This is like endeavoring to repeal the law of gravity, or to annul all human history. (Newton is mentioned here because the denouncers of "Euroculture" declare that the scientific departments, too, must be purged of racism, sexism, and the dread sin of Eurocentrism.)

Much in American education requires improvement. Indeed oppression exists in the typical curriculum; but it is the tyranny of Giant Dullness, not the despotism of White Capitalistic Exploitation. So Multiculturalists' denunciation of existing educational programs sometimes hits the mark. Yet what would the multiculturalist champions of the intellectual rights of blacks, Latinos, and American Indians bestow upon high school and college by way of substitutions? Apparently an omnium-gatherum, in American history, of incidents of oppression of minorities or of "minority" heroism, mingled with ideological denunciations of the American Republic. They would erect historical falsehoods in the interest of equality of condition; they would establish on the American campus a proletarian dictatorship of the mind. In the teaching of literature, they would efface the "Euroculture" of Plato and Aristotle, Dante and Cervantes and Shakespeare, supplanting these old fuddy-duddies with minor writers of approved "minority" affiliations, and feminist ideologues of the present century. As for English literature, or American literature in the British tradition, the radicals would chuck it all down the memory-hole—except for such "workers in the dawn" writing as might seem sufficiently denunciatory of capitalism and white supremacy.

The culture of America is but two centuries old—or little more than three centuries and a half, if we turn back to the earliest English settlements on the Atlantic shore. The culture of Britain is some sixteen centuries old, if we begin with the triumph of the Angles and the Saxons. If Americans lose that British patrimony, they must become barbarians, and on their darkling plains ignorant armies of ideologues may clash by night.

The Case for a Defense of the English-Speaking Cultures

The majority of American citizens nowadays are *not* descended from English-speaking ancestors. They are outnumbered by people descended from German-speaking stock: Germans, Austrians, and German-speakers of central Europe. And the proportion of America's population with Italian, Polish, and other European language-roots bulks large. Spanish was spoken, and often still is spoken, by the parents or the grandparents of the ethnic group most rapidly increasing in the United States—that is, Latin-Americans. Asiatic and African immigrants, fugitives most of them from the twentieth-century Time of Troubles, must acquire some proficiency in the English language, a tongue altogether unrelated to their ancestral languages.

Nevertheless, whatever the racial or ethnic or national origins of Americans, the principal features of the culture within which they have their being are British in origin. It is not possible to participate effectively in American society without acquiring that English-speaking culture. For, as Thomas Sowell (some of whose ancestors were African) remarked recently, "Cultural features do not exist merely as badges of 'identity' to which we have some emotional attachment. They exist to meet the necessities and forward the purposes of human life."[8]

In June 1991, the Social Studies Syllabus Review Committee of the state of New York issued a report embracing the notion of "multicultural education" in public schools and rejecting "previous ideals of assimilation to an Anglo-American model." This Syllabus Review Committee, under the authority of the New York State Board of Regents, approved a new "Curriculum of Inclusion" drafted by Leonard Jeffries, a radical black professor who called the existing syllabus "White Nationalism" and ethnocentric.

Professor Arthur Schlesinger, Jr. had been a member of that Syllabus Review Committee; he dissented strongly from the "multicultural" report that the Committee endorsed. His remarks on the report carry weight:

The underlying philosophy of the report, as I read it, is that ethnicity is the defining experience for most Americans, that ethnic ties are permanent and indelible, that the division into ethnic groups establishes the basic structure of American society and that a main objective of public education should be the protection, strengthening, celebration, and perpetuation of ethnic origins and identities. Implicit in the report is the classification of all Americans according to ethnic and racial criteria.[9]

Similar endeavors to repudiate the long-established common culture of America, rooted in many centuries of thought and experience on either side of the Atlantic, have been militant in states other than New York. Were the zealots of multiculturalism to succeed, Americans of differing ethnic origins would scarcely be able to converse together, let alone work together.

Assailants of "the Anglo-American model" for culture often seem to assume that sweeping aside America's established culture would be merely a matter of public policy, with no consequences except a different teaching in classrooms. Thomas Sowell refutes that assumption:

Cultures exist to serve the vital practical requirements of human life—to structure a society so as to perpetuate the species, to pass on the hard-earned knowledge and experience of generations past and centuries past to the young and inexperienced, in order to spare the next generation the costly and dangerous process of learning everything all over again from scratch through trial and error—including fatal errors.

Cultures exist so that people can know how to get food and put a roof over their heads, how to cure the sick, how to cope with the death of loved ones and how to get along with the living. Cultures are not bumper stickers. They are living, changing ways of doing all the things that have to be done in life.[10]

Professor Schlesinger points out that America's language and political purposes and institutions are derived from Britain: "To pretend otherwise is to falsify history. To teach otherwise is to mislead our students." But he adds that "the British legacy has been modified, enriched, and reconstituted by the absorption of non-Anglo cultures and traditions as well as by the distinctive experiences of American life." Very true that is. Yet the British culture is central in certain ways; the other cultures often are peripheral.

Schlesinger concludes by asking his colleagues "to consider what kind of nation we will have if we press further down the road to cultural separatism and ethnic fragmentation, if we institutionalize the classification of our citizens by ethnic and racial criteria and if we abandon our historic commitment to an American identity. What will hold our people together then?"[11] Amen to that!

In the following several chapters, I discuss the ways in which British culture is central to American society. Should that cultural heritage be long and widely neglected, the American nation would drift toward brutishness in private life, anarchy or the mailed fist in public life.

In four major fashions—folkways, if you will—the British mind and British experience, for more than a dozen generations, have shaped the American culture.

The first of these three ways is the English language and the wealth of great literature in that language. Bestriding the world, that English language should be of even greater advantage to Americans today than it has been in the past.

The second of these ways is the rule of law, American common law and positive law being derived chiefly from English law. This body of laws gives fuller protection to the individual person than does the legal system of any other country.

The third of these ways is representative government, patterned upon British institutions that began to develop in medieval times, and patterned especially upon "the mother of parliaments," at Westminster.

The fourth of these ways is a body of *mores*, or moral habits and beliefs and conventions and customs, joined to certain intellectual disciplines. These compose an ethical heritage. According to Tocqueville, Americans' *mores* have been the cause of the success of the American Republic.

In yet other ways, the United States benefits from a British patrimony: the American economy, for instance, developed out of British experience and precedent; and American patterns of community and of family life are British in considerable part. But time being limited, we confine ourselves here to British beliefs and social institutions of which the influence upon Americans has not much diminished with the elapse of four centuries. They will be rejected by those interesting persons who demand that Swahili, rather than English, be taught in urban schools; but most Americans, today as well as yesteryear, take for granted the patterns of Anglo-American culture that I describe.

A culture is perennially in need of renewal. This book, pointing out the British legacy to the culture of America, is meant as a contribution to that cultural invigoration. A culture does not survive and prosper merely by being taken for granted; active defense always is required, and imaginative growth, too. Let us brighten the cultural corner where we find ourselves. For, as T. S. Eliot remarked more than four decades ago, "Culture may even be described simply as that which makes life worth living."[12]

Notes

1. Christopher Dawson, *Religion and Culture* (London: Sheed and Ward, 1948), 48–49.
2. H. J. Rose, *A Handbook of Latin Literature from the Earliest Times to the Death of St. Augustine* (London: Methuen, 1949), 2, n. 1.
3. T. S. Eliot, *Notes towards the Definition of Culture* (London: Faber and Faber, 1949), 21.
4. Ibid., 26.
5. Ibid., 25.
6. Thomas Molnar, *Twin Powers: Politics and the Sacred* (Grand Rapids: Eerdmans, 1988), 114–15.
7. Eliot, *Notes*, 23.
8. Thomas Sowell, address to the American Enterprise Institute, printed in *The Washington Times*, Tuesday, 28 May 1991, C1, C3.
9. Arthur Schlesinger, Jr., "Toward a Divisive Diversity," *The Wall Street Journal*, Tuesday, 25 June 1991, A18.
10. Sowell, address, C3.
11. Schlesinger, "Toward a Divisive Diversity."
12. Eliot, *Notes*, 27.

2

The Language and the Literature

The Barbarism That Became a High Civilization

More than fifteen centuries ago, the Teutonic peoples called Angles, Saxons, and Jutes commenced their conquest of Britain. A half-century earlier, the Roman legions had been withdrawn from the island; only three years after that, the Goths had sacked Rome itself.

The Romano-British population, Roman in culture, most of them Brittonic (Celtic) in speech, struggled to withstand these grim invaders from across the German Ocean. By the middle of the fifth century of the Christian era, these Angles, Saxons, and Jutes were not pirates or plunderers merely; marauders might have looted and passed away. But these tribesmen meant to take possession of the rich soils of Britain; their conquest was a mass migration westward from the coasts of the Low Countries.

With sword, spear, and axe, the Anglo-Saxons effaced a long-established Latin civilization, putting an end to even the language of the native British people. After a century and a half of fierce inter-mittent fighting, the rude conquerors from the Continent held nearly all of what was to be called England—that is, the land of the Angles.

Then from England the Latin language vanished soon, and presently the Celtic tongues, too, went down to dusty death. The towns of Britain, walled though they were, already had been sacked; and the fine villas of the countryside had been burnt or had fallen, deserted, to ruin. By the early years of the seventh century, the Germanic dialects of the illiterate conquerors prevailed from the Isle of Wight to the Firth of Forth. No man in England could write, except conceivably for a few Romano-Britons spared as slaves; no schools survived. The Anglo-Saxons, so ready of sword, axe, and spear, had cut themselves off

13

from the crumbling civilization of Gaul, Iberia, and Italy; even, indeed, from their rough cousins along the shore of the lands now called the Netherlands, Germany, and Denmark. We call the tongue that had developed among these English folk—after they ceased to communicate with related peoples in the Continent—Old English. It was a language more complex and less serviceable than the Modern English that has been spoken from the beginning of the sixteenth century to the present.

Anglo-Saxons had first come to Britain as mercenaries in the service of Rome, and then in the service of the Romano-British authorities who endeavored, after the withdrawal of the Roman legions, to save their country from destruction. About the middle of the fifth century, these Teutonic soldiers began to rebel against what remained of the old Romano-British order; for their masters no longer could pay the mercenaries. Having gained a foothold in the south of Britain, the Anglo-Saxon warriors fetched over from the Continent many thousands of their kinsfolk, who strove to set down roots in the island.

To these newcomers, many of whom had been dwelling precariously on mounds in the watery waste of Frisia (now a province of the Netherlands), fertile and spacious Britain would have seemed like the Garden of Eden—had these barbarians known the Bible. But they were pagans, unlettered, heavy-handed; they burnt the Christian churches and slew the priests. The new little kingdoms of Angles and Saxons and Jutes grew as the strength of the Romano-British waned. By the year 615, the Anglo-Saxon warriors had pushed back their adversaries to the "Celtic Fringe" of Strathclyde, Pictland, Wales, Devon, and Cornwall.

At the beginning of the seventh century, the Saxon culture was far inferior, in all respects, to what remained of the Roman culture in Gaul, Iberia, and Italy. Yet the English language, with the passing of the centuries, would triumph over all rival tongues to become an international language of poetry, commerce, and statecraft. And Englishmen would extend their dominion, by the eighteenth century, to India, North America, and other distant lands (and yet more regions in the nineteenth century), so that it might be said, "The sun never sets on the British Empire."

About the year A.D. 615, of course this sturdy Anglo-Saxon population of England had no expectation of such a triumph for their language, their commerce, their arms. They were cultivators of the soil, dwelling in rude villages, changing little in language or culture for the first five centuries of their inhabiting of Britain. They seem to have subjugated many of the Romano-British and Celtic inhabitants of Britain; before long those vanquished were using the language of their masters.

As a recent historian of the early English settlements writes, "The material and psychological changes which accompanied the general substitution of a Germanic mode of speech for one based either, as in Gaul, on Vulgar Latin or, as in the Celtic lands, on varieties of the Brittonic tongues, must have had profound consequences for the structure of society in all those parts of the country where it occurred."[1] The barbarians extirpated the Latin-speaking educated and administrative classes; Latin learning and Latin customs vanished as the Roman villas and walled towns crumbled. Not until the year 597, when Saint Augustine (sent from Rome by Pope Gregory the Great) began to convert the southern English to Christianity, was the Latin of the Church heard once more in Britain.[2]

During the eighth and ninth centuries, the terrible Danes came down upon England—first as pirates and ravagers, later to occupy two thirds of the country and eventually to settle down peaceably among people of Anglo-Saxon stock. The Danish tongue being closely related to the Anglo-Saxon (or Old English), the two languages blended in northern England. This fusion simplified the general English tongue, gradually—which became an advantage for the English, long later.

Until the seventh-century Christian missionaries from Ireland (speaking Celtic) began to school the northern English, and the Christian missionaries from Rome (speaking Latin) set to work among the southern English, the Anglo-Saxon peoples had no writing. Scalds and bards chanted or shouted their heroic poems (*Beowulf* the chief of these epics), and recited chronicles of kings. Not until King Alfred, late in the ninth century, directed the translation of some important Latin works into the English of the kingdom of Wessex, and commenced the writing of the *Anglo-Saxon Chronicle*, did a written prose literature begin to develop.

In the course of five centuries and longer, only modest progress toward a high culture had been made among English-speaking folk.[3] Into this rather somnolent culture of the English there burst, in the year

1066, the Norman power. French-speaking William the Conqueror, swiftly mastering the whole of England, stripped the Saxon nobles and the Saxon Church of their powers, their honors, and their lands. Norman French promptly became the language of the court, of the king's vassals who now were given power almost absolute in every shire, and of vernacular literature. Only the peasantry, after the Norman Conquest, clung to English speech. In the twelfth century it was said that two languages were spoken in the kingdom of England: Latin for the learned, French for the vulgar. No one worth mentioning still spoke the despised English.[4]

Nevertheless, this seemingly dreadful blow to the English language paradoxically hastened the efficient development of that tongue. Not many years after the Conquest, Old or Early English gave way to the speech called Middle English. (Some philologists, however, argue that the triumph of Middle English did not occur until after the year 1200.) The Normans, Logan Pearsall Smith writes,

> did not, like the Danes, break up or confuse Anglo-Saxon by direct conflict; but their domination, by interrupting the tradition of the language, by destroying its literature and culture, by reducing it to the speech of uneducated peasants, simply removed the conservative influence of education, and allowed the forces which had been long at work to act unchecked; and English, being no longer spoken by the cultivated classes or taught in the schools, developed as a popular language with great rapidity.[5]

In other words, during a period when English learning was repressed, the grammatical restrictions of the Old English, spoken before the Norman Conquest, were relaxed; for unlettered peasants are little concerned for proper grammar. Paradoxically, then, the Anglo-Saxon language after the Conquest became a freer and more flexible tongue. During that time many French words were "borrowed" by the English speakers—or, to write more accurately, words from the dialect of French then spoken in Normandy became permanently incorporated in the changing English language. And many Latin words, which Norman French had borrowed earlier, also passed into the Middle English that was taking form. French imagination subtly woke the English mind, leading presently to high poetry and prose in Middle English.

For three centuries after the Conquest, Norman French was the official tongue of the court, the parliament, the law, and the schools.

Yet by the year 1400, English regained its old dignity, supplanting French at every level of society. Trevor Rowley summarizes this resurrection of a submerged literature:

> Although the French language had a considerable influence on the development of English it did not replace it, and eventually the descendants of the Norman aristocracy spoke English. . . . The areas covered by "borrowed" words from French in the English language tells much of the social pattern imposed by the Conquest. There was heavy borrowing in administration, government and law, and the legal vocabulary became almost exclusively French. There was also considerable influence in matters concerning the social organization of the upper classes. In literary, architectural and cultural fields the terminology is also predominantly French. It is not surprising that the language of commerce and of town life should, too, have become mainly French. It must, however, be emphasized that these changes were not sudden and some of the transference did not take place until the twelfth and thirteenth centuries when . . . French survived as the courtly language. In striking contrast to this strong permeation in the language of the upper echelons of society there was relatively little influence in the more mundane activities where the vast majority of the population worked. There was very little borrowing of agricultural, industrial or fishing terms. This reinforces the view that the Normans brought little new in the way of technology, or even organizational change in contrast to commerce, trade and administration.[6]

Why was it that English, in the long run, triumphed over French? Because the Norman newcomers, warlike and energetic though they were, formed but a small minority of England's population during the eleventh and twelfth centuries; and intermarriage reduced the barriers between Norman and Saxon stocks. Moreover, the Norman and Angevin kings had to reckon with a free Saxon peasantry, not serfs or slaves, whose support in arms was required for the realm's wars with France, Scotland, Wales, and Ireland. Also the interests of kings and nobles in the affairs of the Continent diminished with the passing of the years, so that the French tongue lost something of its immediate usefulness. Even England's kings came to speak English habitually.

Once more English books were written. Norman domination had enriched the English language; for one thing, the bold challenge of Norman-French culture roused up a life-renewing response from speakers and writers of English.

This not being a book of philology and etymology, the changes in inflections, vocabulary, sentence structure, and other elements that shaped Middle English during the Middle Ages cannot be analyzed at length here. It must suffice to say that this enlivened language of

English, this Middle English, was the medium of a great poet, Geoffrey Chaucer, whose *Canterbury Tales* still are read and taught—even
though one must acquire the knack of reading Chaucer's English of
yesteryear—wherever English is now spoken.

Seven centuries after he wrote, the *Canterbury Tales* still inform the
world that life is worth living. As G. K. Chesterton comments, "Those
strangely fanatical historians, who would darken the whole medieval
landscape, have to give up Chaucer in despair; because he is obviously
not despairing. His mere voice hailing us from a distance has the
abruptness of a startling whistle or halloo, a blast blowing away all
their artificially concocted atmosphere of gas and gloom."[7]

As Dante's *Divine Comedy*, nearly a century earlier, had nobly
expressed the moral imagination of medieval times, so Chaucer's *Canterbury Tales* represented the wit and wisdom of the Middle Ages, the
Ages of Faith—an era already dissolving as Chaucer wrote.[8] Hard of
Chaucer's heels arrived a changed climate of opinion, bringing with it
a new mode of expression: Modern English.

The Virtues of a Language Terse and Forceful

What we write and speak today, Modern English, arose about the
year 1500—even if a good many readers near the end of this twentieth
century may experience difficulties in apprehending the poetry of the
early decades of the sixteenth century. The Renaissance of the fifteenth
and sixteenth centuries had brought to English literature a vastly enlarged knowledge of the Greek classics and also of Roman literature;
thus many Greek words were borrowed by the English, and more Latin
terms and phrases were incorporated. Modern English, as British commerce crossed the seas and the New World beckoned, became a language terse and forceful when compared with other tongues. A major
advantage enjoyed by the British of the past five centuries has been its
simplicity and directness. (In some Indic tongues, to express a concept
or to complete a narration requires several times as much declamation
or composition as is required in Modern English.)

"Simplicity of language is, in fact, like other kinds of simplicity, a
product of a high civilization," Logan Pearsall Smith points out, "not
a primitive condition; and the advance of analysis, the creation of
words expressing abstract relations, is one of the most remarkable

triumphs of the human intellect."[9] Analytical, direct, and economical, English prose well met the needs of the Age of Expansion across the seas.

Otto Jespersen, the great Danish authority on the English language, declares that "English is more masculine than most languages." He means that it is concise and terse. He finds it marked by a certain sobriety of expression. The word order of English sentences helps listener and reader to apprehend swiftly: "Words in English do not play at hide-and-seek, as they often do in Latin, for instance, or in German, where ideas that by right belong together are widely sundered in obedience to caprice or, more often, to a rigorous grammatical rule." English grammar is free from pedantry:

> The French language is like the stiff French garden of Louis XIV, while the English is like an English park, which is laid out seemingly without any definite plan, and in which you are allowed to walk everywhere according to your own fancy without having to fear a stern keeper enforcing rigorous regulations. The English language would not have been what it is if the English had not been for centuries great respecters of the liberties of each individual and if everybody had not been free to strike out in new paths for himself.[10]

Borrowing from several other languages, English near the end of the twentieth century contains some half-million words—many more than does any other tongue, modern or ancient; it is rich in synonyms, to the advantage of English verse. It is a swift and accurate means of communication. Henry Alexander writes that the simplicity of its formal pattern enables English to work best in practice: "English prefers to travel lightly; it gets to its destination . . . like the lightly-burdened traveller, rather more comfortably and rapidly."[11]

Logan Pearsall Smith sums up the virtues of the English language, which he finds

> a methodical, energetic, business-like and sober language, that does not care much for finery and elegance, but does care for logical consistency and is opposed to any attempt to narrow-in life by police regulations and strict rules either of grammar or of lexicon. As the language is, so also is the nation,
>
> > *For words, like Nature, half reveal*
> > *And half conceal the Soul within.*[12]

In large part a product of the Renaissance of learning and emotion that had spread from Italy to Britain, Modern English became a language both of poetry and of commerce, at once imaginative and practical. Soon it crossed the high seas.

Modern English, in short, took form simultaneously with the opening of the New World soon to be called America. Columbus had reached the West Indies in 1492; John Cabot, under patent from Henry VII of England, had discovered the coast of North America in 1497. Much was changing in the world by the year 1500 besides the changing English language. The medieval order was passing away swiftly; soon such pilgrimages as that of Chaucer's *Canterbury Tales* would be denounced by Reformers as banefully superstitious.

Throughout the reign of Elizabeth I (1558-1603), English poetry, drama, and prose took on a splendor exceeding the attainments of French, Italian, and Spanish literature during that grand age. The genius of William Shakespeare, philosophical dramatist, won the admiration of all Europe. In Shakespeare's plays, Modern English achieved its perfection.

It was an age of audacity in politics, in war, in literature. Sir Walter Ralegh—poet, courtier, soldier, adventurer, historian, colonizer, much favored by Queen Elizabeth—sufficiently illustrates that versatile audacity. King James I, Elizabeth's successor, imprisoned him in the Tower of London, on a charge of treason; and in 1618 Ralegh was beheaded. In the Tower he had written his *History of the World*; and also verses, of which "The Lie" is a specimen of the heroic and eloquent character of that epoch. Here are four stanzas of the poem's thirteen.

> *Go, soul, the body's guest*
> *Upon a thankless arrant.*
> *Fear not to touch the best;*
> *The truth shall be thy warrant.*
> *Go, since I needs must die,*
> *And give the world the lie.*
>
> *Say to the court, it glows*
> *And shines like rotten wood;*
> *Say to the church, it shows*
> *What's good, and doth no good:*
> *If church and court reply,*
> *Then give them both the lie.*

* * *

Tell zeal it wants devotion;
Tell love it is but lust;
Tell time it meets but motion;
Tell flesh it is but dust:
  And wish them not reply,
  For thou must give the lie.

* * *

So when thou hast, as I
Commanded thee, done blabbing
Because to give the lie
Deserve no less than stabbing,
  Stab at thee he that will—
  No stab thy soul can kill.

Walter Ralegh it had been who first had endeavored to found English colonies in America—at Roanoke Island, on the coast of Virginia, in 1585 and 1587; both attempts had been short-lived, but soon Ralegh would have emulators.* In 1607 a permanent English settlement was established at Jamestown, in Virginia; the bold Captain John Smith, who commanded its train-band, would become America's first English author. Ralegh's *History of the World* would be read by a great many colonists all along the Atlantic seaboard.[13]

In 1620, the English Pilgrims settled at Plymouth, in what is now Massachusetts. In language and literature, Virginia and Massachusetts (and presently eleven other colonies) transplanted England to the eastern shore of America. Almost four centuries later, that language and that literature remain the footing for the culture of some two hundred and eighty million North Americans.

In the course of a thousand years, the language that once had been called Anglo-Saxon had developed into the splendid poetry and prose of Edmund Spenser, Sir Philip Sidney, William Shakespeare, Christopher Marlowe, Ben Jonson, Walter Ralegh, Thomas Fuller, and other writers of genius. The English literature that had commenced with Caedmon's paraphrases of the Scriptures and Bede's *Ecclesiastical History* had culminated, during the reigns of Elizabeth I and James I,

---

*Sir Walter's name is spelt "Raleigh" in some books; he himself signed his name variously on various occasions.

in tragedies and comedies and histories that would be enacted on the stages of many lands for centuries to come; in sonnets and lyrics of high beauty and pathos; in essays and theological works of much penetration. Upon this literary diet the early English settlers in North America were nurtured—and upon English translations of Greek and Roman works, too. True, during the early decades of colonization the planters and fishermen and lumbermen and distillers of the New World were more immediately interested in religious tracts, and in publications of some immediate usefulness, than in works of humane letters. Yet before very long the southern colonies, and then New England, commenced to apprehend the great imaginative literature of the sixteenth and seventeenth centuries. The early colonists knew, too, great Roman and Greek literature.

As Wallace Notestein remarks, "The settlers in the American colonies might have been supposed to be too near the instant need of things to have shown interest in classical works. But they carried books with them, and not only about theology and law. From almost the beginning a few of them had Latin books on their shelves."[14]

French publications of the seventeenth and eighteenth centuries were not very widely read in America; nor were German. But every important book published at London, Edinburgh, Bristol, or Dublin found its way to British North America during the closing quarter of the seventeenth century and the whole of the eighteenth century, sometimes in large quantities. And printing presses were at work in the American seaboard towns by the middle of the seventeenth century.

The book that was to exert a stronger influence than any other in America was not published until 1611, a few years after the first Virginian settlement: the "King James" translation of the Bible, the Authorized Version prepared by English scholars for King James I.[15] Read from American pulpits and in the great majority of American households during colonial times, the Authorized Version shaped the style, informed the intellect, affected the laws, and decreed the morals of the North American colonies.

The King James Bible, Barrett Wendell observes, "is probably the greatest masterpiece of translation in the world; it has exercised on the thought and the language of English-speaking peoples an influence which cannot be overestimated."[16] After the Bible, the book most widely read in seventeenth- and eighteenth-century North America was John Bunyan's great Christian allegory *The Pilgrim's Progress* (published in 1678). That fable has been called "the first English novel"—and, like certain other major novels, it presents enduring truths in the guise of fiction. Washington Irving and Nathaniel Hawthorne, and other American men of letters during the first half of the nineteenth century, would keep the memory of Bunyan green.

America was settled during, or shortly after, the greatest period of English imaginative literature. "The glory of the English Renaissance was the literature produced in the reign of Elizabeth: the epic poetry of Edmund Spenser, the rich cadences of Christopher Marlowe, the dramatic blank verse of William Shakespeare, the graceful sonnets of a Philip Sidney or a Walter Ralegh, and the prose and verse of a score of other writers, who, in a less distinguished age, would have shone as stars of the first magnitude"—so Louis B. Wright declares. "The literary brilliance of the Elizabethans outlived the Queen who gave her name to the age, and the afterglow of that period lasted far into the seventeenth century."[17]

Between the year 1600 and the year 1700, twelve of Britain's North American colonies were established. In the seventeenth century, three of the greatest of English men of letters roused the imagination: Shakespeare, copies of whose plays might be found in American frontier cabins; John Milton, creator of the grandest English epic, *Paradise Lost*; and John Dryden, master of the heroic couplet and critic who gave permanent form to modern English prose.

Throughout the eighteenth century, too, the Americans read great English authors: the essays of Joseph Addison, the criticism of Samuel Johnson and his moral essays, the speeches of Edmund Burke. They became familiar also with the philosophers and the novelists of England and Scotland and Ireland. Right down to the fighting at Lexington, Concord, and Boston in 1775, Americans looked to London, Edinburgh, and Dublin for literary and philosophical judgments. British periodicals—*The Gentleman's Magazine, The Spectator, The Rambler, The Annual Register*—much influenced Americans' opinions.

Of the books written in the thirteen colonies during that age, only Benjamin Franklin's autobiography is widely read today. The sermons of Jonathan Edwards (1703-1758) are the most enduring theological writings of colonial times. Much interesting writing was in the form of journals: among the more important of journal authors were John

Winthrop, founder of Massachusetts Bay Colony, whose "history" covered the years 1630-1649; William Byrd of Virginia, his diaries and "history" extending from 1709 to 1740, but chiefly concerned with Virginia and North Carolina in 1728; and John Woolman, a Quaker of New Jersey, who travelled about the colonies from 1743 to 1772.

So for a century and a half the American colonists read books written in Britain, chiefly—and read them with very close attention. From the beginning of settlement, Louis B. Wright points out, Americans

> envisioned in America a projection of English civilization; and they were determined that learning and the cultivation of the mind and spirit should not perish in the wilderness. Books which provided guidance in the way of life that the colonists were marking out for themselves predominated, therefore, in their literary preferences. . . . That reading should tend toward instruction in the proper way of life was the persistent advice of all serious writers, both secular and ecclesiastical. . . . The colonists, like their kindred in England, no doubt read Raleigh's history, not merely as a compendium of facts about the ancient world, but also as a source of political and moral truths."[18]

The Conjunction of English and American Literature

Not until the nineteenth century would American authors begin to be much read in Britain. But once the books of Washington Irving, Nathaniel Hawthorne, and James Fenimore Cooper came from the press, and were cordially read and much reprinted in Britain, the bond between the British culture and the American culture was reinforced: a common literature softened on either side the bitter memories of the War of Independence and the War of 1812.

Despite the steady growth of American publishing after the year 1700, British books and British critical judgments loomed very large indeed in the United States until the middle of the nineteenth century. In what is called the Romantic Age, nearly every well-schooled American read much of Walter Scott, William Wordsworth, Samuel Taylor Coleridge, Lord Byron, Percy Bysshe Shelley, John Keats, and the other principal British authors of the time; according to Mark Twain, Sir Walter Scott's medievalism fortified political opinion in the South.

During the reign of Queen Victoria, American readers eagerly acquired the novels of Charles Dickens, William Makepeace Thackeray, Anthony Trollope, Robert Louis Stevenson, and other English and

Scottish writers; they knew well the poetry of Robert Browning, Lord Tennyson, Edward Fitzgerald, Matthew Arnold, Dante Gabriel Rossetti. School anthologies in the United States were thickly packed with selections from such British authors of verse and prose—to which were added, as a distinctive American literature developed, the poets and essayists of New England, the Middle States, and the South.[19]

British folk tale and fairy tale rejoiced American children until very recent decades. John Ruskin's tale *The King of the Golden River*, with its two Black Brothers transformed into two black stones because they had not charity, was printed in full in most readers for American primary schools, until the First World War swept away much else. Between the same textbook covers might be printed Washington Irving's story of the Headless Horseman, or the tale of Rip Van Winkle. Anthologists and teachers took it for granted that there existed no wall of separation between British literature and American literature.

By 1901, the year in which Queen Victoria's reign ended, the United States was nearly so great a power in the world as was the British Empire; yet these two powers were not hot rivals, for a common culture joined them in affection; and a common body of literature reminded them very frequently of their kinship. Eight years after Victoria's death, Barrett Wendell, professor of English at Harvard College (an institution founded in 1638 by John Harvard, from Southwark, on the south bank of the Thames), published *A Literary History of America*, a book still well worth reading. In his concluding chapter, Wendell described with strong feeling the ties of literature and law that had joined America and Britain for three centuries past:

The literary history of America is the story, under new conditions, of those ideals which a common language has compelled America, almost unawares, to share with England. . . . The ideals which for three hundred years America and England have cherished, alike yet apart, are ideals of morality and of government—or right and of rights. Whoever has lived his conscious life in the terms of our language, so saturated with the temper and the phrases both of the English Bible and of English Law, has perforce learned that, however he may stray, he cannot escape the duty which bids us do right and maintain our rights. General as these phrases must seem—common at first glance to the serious moments of all men everywhere,— they have, for us of English-speaking race, a meaning peculiarly our own. Though Englishmen have prated enough and to spare, and though Americans have declaimed about human rights more nebulously still, the rights for which Englishmen and Americans alike have been eager to fight and to die are no prismatic fancies gleaming through clouds of conflicting logic and metaphor; they are that living body of customs and duties and privileges, which a process very like physical growth has made the vital condition of our national existence. Through immemorial experience, the rights which we most jealously cherish have proved themselves safely favorable at once to prosperity and to righteousness. . . . In loyalty to this conception of duty, the nobler minds of England and America have always been at one.[20]

As Wendell suggests in the preceding passages, a close connection subsists between a culture's literature and a culture's laws; and also a connection no less close between literature and morals. Such subjects will be explored in later chapters of this book. The language and the literature transmitted to America from Britain carried with them certain assumptions about liberty and order, as expressed through law; also certain assumptions about the human condition, "of moral evil and of good." Highly ethical in significance from the days of Sir Walter Ralegh and Captain John Smith, of John Winthrop and Increase Mather, down to such twentieth-century champions of culture as C. S. Lewis and T. S. Eliot, the body of English literature produced on either shore of the Atlantic still instructs us in what it is to be fully human, the reason restraining will and appetite. Eliot, born in St. Louis and buried in England, is a tall symbol of the literary union and the moral conjunction of the United States and Britain. He reminds us that "the communication of the dead is tongued with fire beyond the language of the living."

The great literature of yesteryear is the communication of the dead to the living; it is the bequest of vanished generations to the generation now quick. Without that inheritance, you and I would be straying in a dark wood, in peril of mires and pitfalls. Through enduring literature, wisdom—the wisdom of the species, the intellectual bank and capital of *homo sapiens*—survives the tooth of Time the Devourer.

In our age when books of every sort are readily available, try to imagine what a good book meant to Americans of the year 1700, say. During the dark hours, no illumination for reading could be had but the candle, the rush light, or the betty oil lamp. Books of any sort were few and costly. There existed no television, no radio, no films in theaters, no videos, no tapes, no airplanes, no railroads, no automobiles. Only through the reading of books might most men and women escape from the provinciality of place and the provinciality of time.

Books in 1700 were eagerly sought after by all who could read; for from books one might learn answers to ultimate questions.

In the year 1992, some Americans abominate the sight of good books; and others shrug their shoulders at *King Lear*, or *The Pilgrim's Progress*, or even *Robinson Crusoe*. Such books, we are told, were written in a foreign land by "dead white males." No doubt; but as Gustave Le Bon insists, "The dead alone give us energy."

Notes

1. J. N. L. Myres, *The English Settlements* (Oxford: Clarendon Press, 1986), xxiv.
2. In Roman Britain (A.D. 43–407, approximately), it appears, only the upper classes spoke Latin as their primary tongue; the majority of the population seem to have reverted to Brittonic speech altogether, by degrees, well after the Emperor Honorius abandoned the defense of Britain. Even at the present day, forms of Gaelic are spoken by small minorities in the west of Scotland and of Ireland, and by many people in Wales; the last speaker of Cornish Gaelic died in the nineteenth century. Today the most numerous speakers of Gaelic are found in the French province of Brittany, to which region many Britons fled across the Channel in the course of the Anglo-Saxon mass migration to Britain itself.
3. In recent years several perceptive books about Anglo-Saxon England, profiting from much recently disinterred archeological evidence, have been published. Among them are these: J. N. L. Myres, *The English Settlements*, see note 1; Martyn J. Whittock, *The Origins of Britain, 410-600* (Totowa, N.J.: Barnes & Noble, 1986); Henry Marsh, *Dark Age Britain: Sources of History* (New York: Dorset Press, 1970); Catherine Hills, *Blood of the British, from Ice Age to Norman Conquest* (London: George Philip, 1986). The famous Victorian *History of the Anglo-Saxons* (1876) by Sir Frances Palgrave is available in a recent reprint (New York, Dorset Press, 1989). The most famous and influential study in this field is Sir Frank Stenton's *Anglo-Saxon England, 550-1087* (Oxford: Clarendon Press, third edition, 1971).
4. For a close examination of Norman mastery, see Frank Stenton, *William the Conqueror and the Rule of the Normans* (New York: Barnes & Noble, 1966).
5. Logan Pearsall Smith, *The English Language* (London: Williams and Norgate, 1912), 20–21.
6. Trevor Rowley, *The Norman Heritage, 1066-1700* (London: Routledge and Kegan Paul, 1983), 180–81.
7. G. K. Chesterton, *Chaucer* (London: Faber & Faber, 1902), 183.
8. An interesting picture of England and English culture at the end of the Middle Ages is Caxton's compilation *The Description of Britain*. William Caxton was the first English printer; he published his *Description*, edited from earlier sources, in 1480. A handsome recent version, well illustrated, is Caxton, *The Description of Britain, a Modern Rendering by Marie Collins* (London: Sidgwick and Jackson, 1988; also an American distribution by Weidenfeld & Nicholson, New York).
9. Logan Pearsall Smith, *The English Language*, 13.

10. Otto Jespersen, *Growth and Structure of the English Language* (New York: Appleton-Century, fourth edition, 1923), 5–16.
11. Henry Alexander, *The Story of Our Language* (revised edition, Garden City, N.Y.: Anchor Books, 1969), 27.
12. Smith, *The English Language*, 17.
13. A recent life, well illustrated, of Ralegh is John Winton's *Sir Walter Ralegh* (New York: Coward, McCann, and Geoghegan, 1975).
14. Wallace Notestein, *The English People on the Eve of Colonization, 1603-1630* (New York: Harper and Brothers, 1954), 31, n. 15.
15. For knowledge of the making of the King James Version, consult Ward Allen, editor and translator, *Translating for King James*, notes made by John Bois, one of James's translators (Nashville: Vanderbilt University Press, 1969).
16. Barrett Wendell, *A Literary History of America* (New York: Charles Scribner's Sons, 1909), 5.
17. Louis B. Wright, *The Atlantic Frontier: Colonial American Civilization, 1607-1763* (New York: Alfred A. Knopf, 1947), 29–30.
18. Louis B. Wright, *The First Gentlemen of Virginia: Intellectual Qualities of the Early Colonial Ruling Class* (Charlottesville: The University Press of Virginia, 1964), 128, 131.
19. See, for instance, Newcomer and Andrews (eds.), *Twelve Centuries of English Poetry and Prose* (Chicago: Scott, Foresman and Company, 1910).
20. Wendell, *A Literary History*, 521–22.

3

The Supremacy of Law

The Advantages of the Common Law

The purpose of any system of law is to keep the peace; that is, to prevent or discourage violence and fraud, so that people may live in community with some security, maintaining a common culture of many benefits. The system of law that developed in England, from the latter half of the eleventh century to the present, has been more successful in keeping the peace than have been the laws of other cultures and nations.

England's rather elaborate juridical structure is founded upon what is called "the Common Law." (The word *common* here signifies that this body of laws is recognized and enforced throughout all the land, rather than being merely local law or custom; also it signifies that "the law is no respecter of persons," all orders and classes, including kings, being subject to its rules — "equality before the law.") England's common law is the footing for American law as well, and for all major English-speaking countries — with the interesting exception of Scotland, where the legal system for the most part is civil law, Roman in its roots.

Often this common law is called "unwritten law," meaning that it does not consist of written statutes promulgated by a legislature or a monarch. No formal published code of common law exists, on either side of the Atlantic. Instead, the common law is "judges' law," made up of the accumulated decisions of common-law judges over a long period of time. Although this common law is founded in considerable part upon long-established customs — including antique Anglo-Saxon customs and, in America, colonial customs — it is not simply "customary law." Instead, it amounts to the considered judgments of able judges, in a multitude of cases.

So statutory law, either side of the ocean, is one thing; common law, another. Also the common law must be distinguished from the civil law, derived from Roman law, that prevails in the greater part of the European continent. Differences between these two systems will be touched upon later in this chapter.

In all of the fifty United States except Louisiana (which has a form of civil law, derived from the French and Spanish colonizers of that region), the common law borrowed from England still remains in effect, alongside the statutes—written laws—of state legislatures. When a judge in some American state tries a case at common law, he is expected to base his decision upon legal precedents set by earlier common-law judges—possibly by judges in some other state, perhaps in some other country.

This is the doctrine of *stare decisis*—"to stand by decided cases." An "organic" development that respects precedents and customs, this common law grew up in England not long after the Norman Conquest; and it has functioned so well for nearly a thousand years that almost nobody nowadays in the English-speaking world proposes to supplant the common law by some more "rational" system.

Thus the common law is "case law," founded in the beginning upon judges' interpretations of customs generally accepted as fair and reasonable through England. Common-law judges have available a mass of previous decisions upon which to base their own rulings; and for the past century and more, since the old courts of Equity were united with common-law courts, common-law judges have possessed a considerable latitude in adapting old common law to changed circumstances; thus a body of principles that developed in medieval times still can serve to govern commercial contracts, criminal offenses, real-property transactions, and many other complex matters of litigation in the twentieth century. Here is a working description.

The common law is a body of general rules prescribing social conduct.

The common law has developed its principles from the grounds of decisions in actual legal controversies ("case law"), not from a sovereign's edicts or a legislature's enactments.

The common law empanels a jury, originally composed of "twelve good men and true," to determine guilt or innocence, or else the rightfulness or unrightfulness of claims.

The common law gives to those who come within its jurisdiction privileges unknown in civil or Roman law, where generally the interest of the State looms first. Under the common law, for instance, a defendant cannot be compelled to testify, if he chooses to remain silent; he is saved from self-incrimination. A complex system of writs, under common law, has made access to justice relatively easy for the individual. No person may be imprisoned without a warrant, and the accused must be tried speedily: "justice delayed is justice denied." Civil rights are protected by juries, in the sense that a state-appointed judge cannot enforce arbitrarily the will of a political regime without the sanction of twelve (or fewer) independent citizens. Even the state's officers, if they interfere unlawfully with subjects' or citizens' rights, may be sued for damages under the common law, or perhaps charged in a common-law court with criminal actions. In all this, the "private law" called "common law" secures the private person against arbitrary actions by the possessors of power.

The common law is distinguished from civil-law proceedings also by the common law's "adversary" contests in the courtroom. In European civil law, as systems of law developed during early medieval times, the accused person was presumed to be guilty as charged by a prosecutor; the judge determined the issue to be settled in a case at law; and in other ways a court of law was an instrument of state authority. But under the common law of England, the plaintiff and the defendant, or the prosecutor and the defendant, are regarded as adversaries, on an equal footing. Their lawyers define the issue to be settled, while the judge remains neutral. A defendant in a criminal case is presumed to be innocent unless the evidence proves him to be guilty beyond a reasonable doubt.

The common law is founded upon the assertion of the supremacy of law: that is, as Bracton and other medieval scholars in the law expressed it, even the king himself was "under the law." As one recent writer puts it, "The supremacy of law implies that all agencies of government must act upon established principles; even the highest bodies and officials are not permitted to act upon arbitrary will or caprice. The supremacy of law means that all the acts of government agencies are subject to examination in the courts, which are compelled in their turn to follow established procedures, 'due process', and to reach decisions guided not by whim but by generally accepted principles and sound reason."[1]

This principle of the supremacy of law, or the rule of law, often expressed by the phrase "a government of laws, not of men," well suited the Americans of the seventeenth and eighteenth centuries, living as they did remote from kings, peers, and bishops. The common law itself, adapted to American circumstances, functioned in British North America—not that many of the colonists possessed detailed knowledge of it.

We have said that the common law has been called "unwritten law," and so it was in the beginning. But soon the decisions of common-law judges began to be set down as records of judgments, from which precedents applicable to new cases of a similar character might be ascertained. Rather than "unwritten law," really, common law may be described as noncodified law. Formal statutes of a state ordinarily are embodied in a formal legal code; but common law, based upon a multitude of precedents rather than upon statutory codes or legal theories, is "judge-made law." It has grown out of practical contests at law, occurring over the centuries. There exists no need for ratification of the common law by the Crown in Parliament, or by Congress, or by state legislatures. Common-law judges are expected to abide by the accumulated experience of many courts, in which learned judges have interpreted and applied ancient customs generally believed to be just. (For instance, the common-law ruling that a man is held responsible for debts incurred by his wife as his household partner.) Where the common law prevails, people will be able to act on the assumption that the law will not alter capriciously from year to year.

Common-law judges, and the lawyers in their courts, need to be people of much knowledge. For, as J. C. Gray pointed out in 1916, with respect to records of common-law cases, "At the end of the eighteenth century the total number of printed volumes of reported cases in England, Ireland, the English colonies, and the United States of America was two hundred and sixty. At the end of the year 1865 they had increased more than twelve-fold to over three thousand, not including the Indian Reports, and at the end of the nineteenth century the published reports of decisions in the United States alone were contained in about six thousand volumes."[2] Of course a century later the volumes of such reports line whole corridors of much length in the basements of great law libraries.

The common-law judge is required to hear the arguments of opposing litigants, either of whom will cite precedents favoring his own claim; and the judge is to decide in favor of the litigant whose lawyer has most convincingly demonstrated that precedent stands on his side. This "adversary relationship," in which the court treats both litigants as if they were equal parties (even though one of them may be the State) and maintains impartiality, contrasts strongly with the Civil Law (or Roman Law), in which the judge aggressively seeks out the truth of the matter; and, if a public prosecutor is one of the litigants, the burden of proof is thrust upon the accused, the defendant.

Another distinguished feature of the common law is its employment of a jury, usually of a dozen persons; for in courts of another sort, operating on other juridical principles, decisions are handed down by a judge or a panel of judges. In modern times, the fact-finding jury is peculiar to England and those countries, the United States eminent among them, that have emulated the English common-law system. Serving on juries became a powerful instrument for instructing the public in the nature of law. Also jury service is a form of popular representation in public affairs: one important reason, this, why representative government arose first in England, for participation in common-law juries taught free men how to assert their part in public concerns.

These and other advantages of the common-law courts of England brought about a most strong attachment of the English people to the common law, as the guardian of their ancient customs, their property, and their liberties. Indeed, during the fourteenth century—so Edward S. Corwin notes—the common-law courts loomed larger in public approbation than did Magna Carta, the Great Charter of 1215, the old symbol of order and freedom:

> At a time when people did not know from day to day whether Lancaster or York sat on the throne [during the Wars of the Roses], the common-law courts continued for the most part in the discharge of their proper business. The result was that, as Englishmen recognized in the daily practice of the courts an actual realization of most that Magna Carta had symbolized, they transferred to the common law as a whole the worship which they had so long reserved more especially for the Charter. The common law, infused with the principles of Magna Carta, came to be regarded as *higher law* . . .[3]

And so the common law came to be regarded by most Americans. On the eve of the War of Independence, the First Continental Congress' *Declaration and Resolves* (14 October 1774) "Resolved, that the respective colonies are entitled to the common law of England, and more especially to the great and inestimable privilege of being tried by their peers of that vicinage, according to the course of that law."[4]

The Patriots were asserting their claim to enjoy what Edmund Burke called "the chartered rights of Englishmen"—not the abstract claims of perfect liberty that would be asserted fifteen years later by French revolutionaries. Rooted in custom and ancient usage, the Common Law's purpose was to work for social harmony, not for social revolution. The American Revolution did not sever the links between British law and American law; rather, the American Republic added more chapters to the complex history of common law.[5]

Blackstone and America's Laws

Between 1765 and 1769, while North American subjects of George III vehemently were making known their displeasure with the policies of the king's ministers, William Blackstone published the four volumes of his *Commentaries on the Laws of England*. Those well-written volumes swiftly became known to leading Americans, an appetite for knowledge of the law being widespread in the thirteen colonies. The first Vinerian professor of law at Oxford University, a Tory in politics, Blackstone (knighted in 1770) had little sympathy for the Patriot cause in America. But promptly his *Commentaries* won popularity and immense influence across the Atlantic, as well as in Britain. An American edition of his work was printed at Philadelphia in 1771-72; St. George Tucker, a distinguished Virginian jurist, published in 1803 an annotated American edition of the *Commentaries*, which affected American law and political thought for a good while. A most able exponent of the common law, Sir William came to exercise even more influence in America than in Britain.

There exist three ways to approach law: first, historically; second, systematically and analytically; third, the deontological or ethical approach, in which one considers society's needs and asks how far the law is adequate to satisfy those needs. Blackstone employed all three methods, sometimes combining them, on other occasions utilizing them separately.

Blackstone explained society's need for jurisprudence, believing that law must be "not a transient sudden order from a superior to or concerning a particular person; but something permanent, uniform, and universal."[6] He agreed with Adam Smith's definition of jurisprudence as "the theory of the rules by which civil government ought to be directed. It attempts to shew the foundation of the different systems of government in different countries and to shew how far they are founded in reason. We will find that there are four things which will be the design of every government." These ends are the maintenance of justice and property; the upholding of internal peace through a police force; the defraying of the expense of government through funds obtained from taxes or rent; and the raising of armies to protect the country from foreign enemies.[7]

Blackstone pointed out that several types of law were present in England: natural law, divine law, law of nations, English common law, local customary law, Roman law, ecclesiastical law, the law merchant, statutory law, and equity. Two kinds of law in particular were emphasized by him. As the *Decretum Gratiani*, about the year 1140, had put it: "Mankind is ruled by two laws: Natural Law and Custom." By "custom" is to be understood the "unwritten" common law, which Blackstone made clearer than had anyone before him. Also he discussed natural law, although his apprehension of the law of nature was less lucid than his mastery of the common law.

Blackstone heartily endorsed natural law, calling it the power from which legal concepts draw their authority and force, and to which man-made laws are ultimately responsible. His understanding of the matter came from two principal sources: the Ciceronian and Christian tradition, and the secularized and rationalistic interpretation of Hugo Grotius and Samuel von Pufendorf, in the seventeenth century— theories not always consonant one with the other.

He found in Magna Carta the expression of three absolute rights: life, liberty, and property. He traced back to that Great Charter the doctrine of due process of law. The ancient right to trial by a jury of one's peers was closely examined by Blackstone; and in many other matters, Blackstone on the British Constitution supplied Americans with arguments pertinent to their contest with the Crown in Parliament. They could cite Blackstone for authority that no tax might be imposed upon them, constitutionally, "without the act and consent of their own legislature," and that justice "ought to be equally, freely, and promptly administered."

Most American lawyers of that day having obtained little formal education, the *Commentaries* became the manual through which they acquired firm knowledge of common and natural law, equity, and the chartered rights of Englishmen. Charles Haar puts this succinctly:

> Blackstone supplied a real need in this country. Without a trained bar, lacking a tradition of learning and of legal education, Americans found his exposition overwhelming in force. It was powerful and direct. Its emphasis on natural law fitted in with the peculiar environments of law in America. Because of the *Commentaries*, English common law became also the common law of the United States. To the link of the common language was added that of common legal principles. The *Commentaries* were a conduit of the ideas of Locke and Montesquieu to the framers of the federal and state constitutions. They attained the position of an oracle of the law on which lawyers for generations cut their teeth; mastery of Blackstone was deemed an adequate preparation for the practice of the law.[8]

Before 1771, a thousand sets of Blackstone's volumes were exported from England to the North American colonies. Edmund Burke, in his great Speech on Conciliation in 1775, emphasized the popularity of Blackstone in America: "I hear that they have sold nearly as many of Blackstone's Commentaries in America as in England"—that despite the disparity in population.

The American upper classes read the *Commentaries* because, in Blackstone's words, it is "an undeniable position that a competent knowledge of the laws of that society in which we live is the proper accomplishment of every gentleman and scholar a highly useful, I had almost said essential, part of a liberal and polite education."[9] Indeed most American gentlemen and scholars, during the heated disputes on the eve of the Revolution, made themselves familiar with the *Commentaries*.

The War of Independence over, and the Articles of Confederation having been found in some degree insufficient, in 1787 the infant American Republic set about achieving "a more perfect union." Blackstone's authority loomed large at the Constitutional Convention in Philadelphia.

"The members of the Great Convention were men of the eighteenth century," M. E. Bradford writes, "but of the English and Scottish enlightenment, not the French. They acted within corporate bonds, out of the momentum of a civilization already over one thousand years old when we achieved our national independence."[10] The system of law with which they were familiar was the English common law, chiefly; and its grand interpreter was Sir William Blackstone. The fifty-five delegates to the Convention at Philadelphia were aware, many of them, that there existed three or four different interpretations of the British Constitution: Montesquieu's, Bolingbroke's, Hume's, Blackstone's. The influence of Blackstone's learning is evident in a good many of the debates of the Convention—in Alexander Hamilton's argument against equal representation of the several states in the Congress, for instance; in George Wythe's statement that liberty cannot exist outside society; in Gunning Bedford's case for legislative supremacy; in John Dickinson's and Gouverneur Morris' advocacy of retaining the benefits of the British Constitution.

The Framers' concept of the right to the freedom of the press, so close to Blackstone's principles, may serve to demonstrate that the influence of his *Commentaries* was not diminished by the Revolution.

Liberty of the press was understood by the Framers in Blackstone's terms: that freedom consisted in there being "no previous restraints" (advance censorship) upon publications; but that censure might be exercised when "criminal matter" should be published. Blackstone had declared that a writer might say what he pleased to the public; but for improper, mischievous, or illegal publication, "he must take the consequences of his own temerity" in fine or imprisonment. That is just what is meant by "freedom of the press" in the First Amendment to the Constitution. As Leonard Levy finds, no leading Americans about the time of the Constitution Convention expressed any view of the freedom of the press that differed substantially from Blackstone's.[11]

In short, with Blackstone the word "liberty" had a restricted signification; and in general the Framers of 1787 subscribed to Blackstone's understanding of that word. This concept of liberty was derived from the old doctrine of natural law, in part, although in greater part from English charter and statute and custom; from prescriptive usage in England. Occasionally turning to natural-law doctrines when it seemed necessary, the American leaders, like Blackstone, preferred to appeal to prescription, ancient usage, and legal precedent.

If we turn to protection of property by the laws, a matter of much concern to the Constitutional Convention, we find that here Blackstone was a chief guide, he having pointed out that law was meant in large part to shelter property from rapine and unjust exaction. Blackstone defined property as "that sole and despotic dominion which one man claims and exercises over the external things of the world, in total exclusion of the right of any other individual in the universe."[12] The Framers implicitly accepted this declaration. as well as Blackstone's doctrine that protection of property is a basic reason for the necessity of government. In English law, most real property (estate) had originated from a royal grant. Although American property had developed under English law and had been granted by the Crown or the Crown's agencies or subordinates, nevertheless real property in America was not so deeply rooted in the British past. Neither in Britain nor in America was property in land really regarded as a gift from the sovereign; rather, proprietors took their possession of land as a right. "Though English and Continental theorists had long maintained that property-holding was an unalienable right that was morally and historically antecedent to government, this idea had undergone some important refinements in English law by the time of Blackstone," Forrest McDonald writes. Blackstone states that private property originally was founded in nature, but that "certainly the modifications under which we find it, the method of conserving it in the present owner, and of transmitting it from man to man, are entirely derived from society."[13]

Thus the right to property becomes a civil right, and one that a person acquires by diminishing his "natural" freedom—as he must do if he is to live in any political society. With property established as a civil right, it may be taken from him if he violates the law. Property also may be taken—the power of eminent domain—if the public good seriously so requires, as for the construction of a public road; for this, fair compensation must be granted to the owner of the property. Such concepts from Blackstone were in the minds of the delegates to the Constitutional Convention.

Also Blackstone's commentaries on property entered into discussions at the Constitutional Convention concerning the ownership of property as a qualification for holding public office. Quoting Blackstone's *Commentaries* in his Convention notes, Rufus King emphasized this: "The true reason of requiring any Qualification, with regard to property in votes is to *exclude such as are in so mean a situation* as are presumed to have no will of their own."[14] Blackstone's conservative views influenced a good many delegates. Gouverneur Morris, citing Blackstone during objections to the Convention's compromise on the question of qualifications for voting and holding office, declared roundly, "Give the votes to people who have no property, and they will sell them to the rich who will be able to buy them."[15]

In a good deal else, the authority of Blackstone's *Commentaries* lies behind the Constitution that was written in 1787. Some people profess to detect the influence of John Locke's *Two Treatises on Government* (published in 1689) behind this or that provision of the Constitution; but probably what they discern is Blackstone, one of whose sources was Locke. Public men like the delegates to the Constitutional Convention tend to read books published during their own youth, rather than political tracts published a century earlier.

Be that as it may, Blackstone's *Commentaries on the Laws of England*, more than any other book, ensured some continuity between British and American political and legal institutions. And Blackstone it was who, describing and praising the common law so lucidly, informed Americans of the enduring nature of that system which many Americans, during the War of Independence, had been ready to discard.

During the formative years of the American Republic, Blackstone's great work altogether dominated legal thought. James Wilson, who had been powerful at the Constitutional Convention, aspired to supplant Blackstone's jurisprudence by a democratic study of the law; but his effort did not succeed.[16] In England, during those years, Bentham's new utilitarian jurisprudence in some degree diminished Blackstone's reputation; yet in the United States, nearly every leading scholar in the law adhered to Blackstone.

In Virginia, the jurist St. George Tucker used Blackstone as the text for study of the law at the College of William and Mary; and his own edition of the *Commentaries* related Blackstone to American circumstances. When a boy, John Marshall read Blackstone; and his formal training in the law consisting of merely some weeks of study with George Wythe at Williamsburg, the *Commentaries* in effect sat on the bench of the Supreme Court of the United States while Marshall was chief justice. John Quincy Adams thought the *Commentaries* a "very improper" book for beginning students of the law, but "an inestimable advantage" in the profession. James Kent read the *Commentaries* at the age of fifteen, and was so mightily impressed that he decided to become a man of law; in the fullness of time, he would become the first professor of law at Columbia University and the author of the influential *Commentaries on American Law* (four volumes, 1826-28). Young Joseph Story, studying law in Massachusetts with Samuel Sewall during 1799, was advised to apply himself thoroughly to Blackstone despite some portions of the *Commentaries* being possibly inapplicable to America. The time would come when Story would be appointed an associate justice of the Supreme Court of the United States and would publish his *Commentaries on the Constitution of the United States* (three volumes, 1833), which for half a century would do much to form political and legal opinion in America. James McClellan writes of Story that "the teachings of Blackstone and the advice of Sewall permanently influenced his thinking, and all his life he remained as devout a son of English legal institutions as a Holt, a Mansfield, or a Burke. The fervid radicalism of Jean Jacques would soon be displaced in Story's mind by the unruffled conservatism of Blackstone; and the reckless denunciation of the common law by Story's fellow democrats, countered by Sewall's encomiums, had no discernible effect on his thinking. He readily shared Sewall's belief that "that system of written & unwritten reason which our fathers brought with them to this country and very early adopted as the bond of the social order' was unquestionably 'their noblest inheritance from their native country,'"[17]

In the next generation of Americans, it was so with young Abraham Lincoln, who said of Blackstone's volumes, "The more I read, the more intensely interested I became. Never in my whole life was my mind so thorough absorbed. I read them until I devoured them." From the first stirrings of revolution in America, then, until the Civil War, Blackstone and his disciples Story and Kent dominated legal education; and through Marshall and Story on the Supreme Court, certain of Blackstone's doctrines and interpretations strongly influenced, for several decades, principal decisions of that most powerful of courts.

The Common Law Prevails in the United States

It was with some difficulty that the common law escaped being swept into oblivion, together with the Crown in Parliament's authority, entail and primogeniture, a church by law established, and other English institutions, in consequence of the British military defeat in the autumn of 1781. Anything distinctively English was bitterly unpopular with the more radical Patriots in their hour of victory. Besides, until Blackstone gave the Americans a better understanding of the common law, the system in North America had seemed more suited to the seventeenth century than to the nineteenth. It conflicted with American individualism. It was accused of being "aristocratical." Its centralized courts and costly procedures alarmed rural Americans.

Moreover, the common law was denounced by Thomas Jefferson and his faction. Paris, not London, was for Jefferson the fountain of enlightenment; and radically new doctrines of law were being preached at Paris. Jefferson, who subscribed to the notion that Anglo-Saxon England had enjoyed perfect freedom, knew that the common law, in its beginnings, had been bestowed upon England by the Norman rulers. Let Normans be anathema!

"I consider all the encroachments made on the Constitution heretofore as nothing, as mere retail stuff, compared with the wholesale doctrine that there is a Common Law in force in the United States, of which, and of all the cases within its provisions, their courts have cognizance," Jefferson wrote to Charles Pinckney in October, 1799. The author of the Declaration of Independence complained that "when the honied Mansfieldism of Blackstone became the student's hornbook, from that moment, that profession (the nursery of our Congress) began to slide into toryism." He disliked the breed of lawyers, with their conservative ways.[18]

Yet what alternative existed to the effective restoration—and improvement—of the common law? On what other principles might courts function, unless judges were to judge by their own prejudices and a rude rule of thumb? How might the supremacy of the law be maintained? Lacking any knowledge of a formal code of positive laws—something quite foreign to British or American social experience—how might Americans live securely in community, sheltered by the law from violence and fraud?

In 1811, Jeremy Bentham, Blackstone's mordant critic, wrote to President Madison offering to draw up a complete legal code of the United States—which the eccentric Bentham never had visited; Madison prudently declined this opportunity to sweep away the common law altogether.

The heated American debate about the virtues and failings of the common law continued for four decades—during which an altered but vigorous revised pattern of common law gradually developed in the several states.[19] By the 1830s, when the books of Chancellor Kent and Justice Story had been published, a renewed common law, historically based, applicable to American circumstances, was winning the contest.

"Many things had operated to retard a complete and final reception of the English common law," Roscoe Pound says,

> not the least the example of the French Civil Code, the enthusiasm for things French following the Revolution and in the era of Jeffersonian democracy, and the natural-law idea that a code could be drafted independent of the historical materials of the law and on a basis of pure reason. . . . In 1833 it was still not wholly settled that we should receive the common law in every state but one, and largely in that state [Louisiana]. But Story had begun to write and under his decisive influence the struggle was substantially at an end.[20]

Jefferson's commination notwithstanding, the common law, received from England, guaranteed to the citizen a fuller degree of freedom from arbitrary power than existed elsewhere in the Americas except for Canada (also a common-law country, for the most part); indeed, a personal liberty and security exceeding that of western Europe and the rest of the world. That renewed pattern of common law now extends so far as Hawaii and Alaska.

Several of the protections provided by the common law were incorporated into the Bill of Rights, ratified in 1791. The Federalists had opposed the Bill of Rights amendments on the ground that liberties already were assured by the common law; but in 1791, the survival of the common law had not grown so certain as it would be in 1833.

The Congress and the state legislatures annually grind out a mass of new or amended statutory law. Yet the importance of the common law has not much diminished. Its principles underlie the whole administration of justice in the United States. Still the common law keeps the peace among us, under the supremacy of law; and that is an enduring contribution of British culture to American.

In 1840, Joseph Story, associate justice of the Supreme Court of the United States and simultaneously professor of law at Harvard, published a manual, *A Familiar Exposition of the Constitution of the*

United States, intended for the common reader and for use as a text-book in high schools. Having described how England's common law was introduced into North America, and how its application varied from one colony to another, Story told why the colonists repeatedly had affirmed their right to the common law:

> Thus limited and defined by the colonists themselves, in its actual application, the common law became the guardian of their civil and political rights; it protected their infant liberties; it watched over their maturer growth; it expanded with their wants; it nourished in them that spirit of independence, which checked the first approaches of arbitrary power; it enabled them to triumph in the midst of dangers and difficulties; and by the good providence of God, we, their descendants, are now enjoying, under its bold and manly principles, the blessings of a free and enlightened administration of public justice.[21]

The Supremacy of Law Peculiar to Britannia and Her Daughters

The common law is a means for assuring the supremacy, or the rule, of law—as opposed to an arbitrary domination by the temporary possessors of power. A. V. Dicey distinguishes three conceptions that are characteristic of the rule of law. "We mean, in the first place, that no man is punishable or can be lawfully made to suffer in body or goods except for a distinct breach of law established in the ordinary legal manner before the ordinary Courts of the land," Dicey says. "In this sense the rule of law is contrasted with every system of government based on the excercise by persons in authority of wide, arbitrary, or discretionary powers of constraint."

Such an understanding of the rule of law, Dicey points out, "is peculiar to England, or to those countries which, like the United States of America, have inherited English traditions." Even in western Europe, "the executive exercises far wider discretionary authority in the matter of arrest, of temporary imprisonment, of expulsion from its territory, and the like, than is either claimed or in fact exercised by the government in England."

The second conception upholding the supremacy of law, according to Dicey, is that no man stands above the law; and moreover, in England and the countries that have inherited British law, "that here every man, whatever his rank or condition, is subject to the ordinary law of the realm and amenable to the jurisdiction of the ordinary tribunals." This is "the idea of legal equality, or universal subjection of all classes to one law administered by the ordinary Courts. . . . Every official is under the same responsibility for every act done without legal justification and any other citizen."

The third conception or attribute of the rule of law is that both the "unwritten" British constitution and the written American constitution grew out of old custom, usage, and political tradition, and from judges' common-law decisions. In other words, the rule of law was not ordained in the formal constitution; rather, the constitution itself is an outgrowth of the rule of law. In the American constitution, as in the British, one finds "an absence of those declarations or definitions of rights so dear to foreign constitutionalists." Mere constitutional declarations of rights are worthless unless founded upon "provision of adequate remedies by which the rights they proclaimed might be enforced." (The English and the American writs of habeas corpus were one such important provision.) In revolutionary France, "the Constitution of 1791 proclaimed liberty of conscience, liberty of the press, the right of public meeting, the responsibility of government officials. But there never was a period in the recorded annals of mankind when each and all of these rights were so insecure, one might almost say so completely non-existent, as at the height of the French Revolution." One now may add to Dicey's aside (written about 1884-85) the observation that still worse acts were committed under the Constitution of the Soviet Union, which was no more than a mask for a hideous "dictatorship of the proletariat" — although that unobserved Soviet document bestowed rights most generously. To flourish, the rule of law requires deep roots; mere parchment constitutions are a snare and a delusion.

Most Americans may take for granted their virtual immunity from serious oppression by men in power. As Dicey puts it, "the statesmen of America have shown unrivalled skill in providing means for giving legal security to the rights declared by American constitutions. The rule of law is as marked a feature of the United States as of England."[22]

The Supreme Court of the United States has been America's chief means for giving legal security to rights. Yet without its British roots, the supremacy of law in the United States might be so precarious as attempts to uphold the rule of law have been in the states of Latin America since those countries declared their independence of the Old World.

Notes

1. Arthur R. Hogue, *Origins of the Common Law* (Indianapolis: Liberty Press, 1985), 188–90.
2. John Chipman Gray, *The Nature and Sources of the Law* (New York: Columbia University Press, 1916), 263.
3. Edward S. Crowin, *Liberty Against Government: The Rise, Flowering and Decline of a Famous Judicial Concept* (Baton Rouge: Louisiana State University Press, 1948), 27.
4. See *Documents Illustrative of the Formation of the Union of the American States*, selected, arranged, and indexed by Charles C. Tansill (Washington: Government Printing Office, 1927), 1–5.
5. The long development of the common law in England is treated most authoritatively by Sir William Holdsworth in his *History of English Law* (London: Methuen and Company, fifteen volumes, seventh edition, 1956). See particularly volume II, book III, "The Medieval Common Law"; and volume IV, book IV, "The Common Law and Its Rivals."
6. William Blackstone, *Commentaries of the Laws of England* (Philadelphia: Robert Ball, 4 vols., 1771-72), vol. I, *Of the Rights of Persons*, 44.
7. Adam Smith, *Lectures on Jurisprudence*, edited by R. L. Meek, D. D. Raphael, and P. G. Stein (Indianapolis: Liberty Classics, 1982), 5–7.
8. Charles Haar, preface to Blackstone's *Of Public Wrongs* (vol. IV of Blackstone's *Commentaries*) (Boston: Beacon Press, 1962), xxii–iii.
9. Blackstone, *Commentaries* (edition of 1771), preface to vol. I (earlier, first Vinerian lecture at Oxford).
10. M. E. Bradford, *A Worthy Company* (Marlborough, N. H.: Plymouth Rock Foundation, 1982), viii.
11. See Leonard W. Levy, "From the Revolution to the First Amendment," in *Legacy of Suppression: Freedom of Speech and Press in Early American History* (Cambridge, Mass.: Belknap Press, 1960); and Forrest McDonald, *Novus Ordo Seclorum: the Intellectual Origins of the Constitution* (Lawrence: University Press of Kansas, 1985), 47–50.
12. Blackstone, *Commentaries*, 1771-72, vol. II, *Of the Rights of Things*, 2.
13. Forrest McDonald, *Novus*, 20.
14. See Robert Ernst, *Rufus King: American Federalist* (Chapel Hill: University of North Carolina Press, 1968), 379, n. 2.
15. Max Farrand (ed.), *The Records of the Federal Convention* (New Haven: Yale University Press, 4 vols., 1911-37), vol. II, 203.
16. See James Wilson, *Lectures on Law*, in Robert Green McCloskey (ed.), *The Works of James Wilson* (Cambridge, Mass.: Belknap Press, 2 vols., 1967).
17. James McClellan, *Joseph Story and the American Constitution* (Norman: University of Oklahoma Press, 1971), 14–15.

18. Yet Jefferson shared with Blackstone the erroneous notion that "at a time which was not buried in a mythological past, the Anglo-Saxons had lived under customs and unwritten laws based upon the natural rights of man and permitting the individual to develop freely, normally and happily." (G. Chinard.) See the concluding chapter (vol. IV) of Blackstone's *Commentaries*, "Of the Rise, Progress and Gradual Improvements of the Laws of England"; and Gilbert Chinard, *Thomas Jefferson, the Apostle of Americanism* (Ann Arbor: University of Michigan Press, second edition, 1957), 31–32.

19. Some account of this process of the revival of the common law may be found in Lawrence M. Friedman's *A History of American Law* (New York: Simon & Schuster, 1985), particularly the prologue and part II, chapter I. The process in Massachusetts is detailed in William E. Nelson's *Americanization of the Common Law: The Impact of Legal Change in Massachusetts Society, 1760-1830* (Cambridge, Mass.: Harvard University Press, 1975). (A certain hostility toward the common law runs through this study.) How the writ of habeas corpus came to America is described by William F. Duker in his second chapter of *A Constitutional History of Habeas Corpus* (Westport, Conn.: Greenwood Press, 1980).

20. Roscoe Pound, *The Formative Era of American Law* (Boston: Little, Brown, 1938), 145.

21. Joseph Story, *A Familiar Exposition of the Constitution of the United States* (New York: Harper & Brothers, 1859; reprinted under the title *The Constitution Handbook*: Chicago, Regnery Gateway, 1986), 36.

22. A. V. Dicey, *Introduction to the Study of the Law of the Constitution* (1885 and 1915) (Indianapolis: Liberty Classics, 1982), 110–21.

4

The Heritage of Representative Government

Its Origins

Nearly all Americans nowadays take representative government for granted. It has existed in North America since the early decades of the seventeenth century; nobody proposes its abolition. And yet truly successful representative government is a rare growth, requiring nurture. In its American form, that sort of government is an inheritance from British political experience and usage.

This phrase "representative government" signifies that public affairs are carried on chiefly by an assembly of persons—politicians, we generally call them—who are presumed to sit in the assembly in the stead of a multitude of people who cannot attend personally; such representatives, substituting for their "constituency," holding their proxies, are sent to join the assembly so that somebody will be present to speak and vote on behalf of some district, association, or political/ economic interest-group which wishes (or is required) to participate in public decisions.

Also it is presumed that a genuine and conscientious political representative will always bear in mind the general public interest of his country, his state (in America), his province, his city—not merely the interest of the smaller group of people who sent him to represent them in some public assembly. There exists a difference between a *delegate*, who is expected merely to carry out the specific instructions of the people who chose him, and a true *representative*, who must be allowed to think for himself and to vote as he finds wisest—all on behalf of his constituents, true. But this distinction will be discussed more fully when, near the conclusion of this present chapter, we turn to Edmund Burke's example.

Representative government did not exist, nor was even thought of, in ancient civilizations. In the city-states of the Hellenic and the Roman epochs, a free government was one in which the citizens—or at least the principal men among them—could assemble in a forum, debate public concerns, and vote as individuals. In neither republican Rome or imperial Rome was any attempt made to "represent" the far-flung provinces or even to represent Italy; for during the Republic the government was carried on by the Senate, an aristocratic self-perpetuating body; and during the Empire by the emperors, their power virtually absolute. Greece and Rome aside, most of the world has been ruled, since the beginning of civilization, by kings, small councils of aristocrats or oligarchs, tyrants, military juntas, or ideological fanatics governing through a bureaucracy. This remains true near the end of the twentieth century, although many governments of the 1990s pretend to be representative in some sense. Possibly a renewal of representative government will follow upon the collapse of the Soviet empire in Eastern Europe. Various forms of representative government have been tried; that of the United States, and that of Britain, are the most nearly successful—despite certain grave evidences of social decadence near the end of the twentieth century.

Even though most Americans take no more part in politics than to vote on election days—and on some occasions less than half the electorate trouble themselves to vote—still they know something about forms of representation in politics: the Congress of the United States, the state legislatures, county councils, municipal councils, district school boards, village and township councils. All these institutions can trace their ancestry back to medieval England. So our scene shifts to the thirteenth century.

A few miles from the great royal castle of Windsor, one still can stroll through the meadows of Runnymede, along a quiet reach of the River Thames—where, in the year 1215, English barons compelled King John to sign Magna Carta, the Great Charter in which the king pledged himself to refrain thereafter from certain offenses against his subjects—against the barons in particular. A medieval king had two great duties: maintaining the bed of justice—that is, keeping the peace domestically, through his sheriffs and his courts—and defending the realm against external enemies. As Rebecca West reminds us, Shakespeare (who wrote much about kings) perceived that "a king was a man in a position where it was very difficult and some times impossible for anybody to stop him from doing as he liked, and where it was certain that at some time or another he would choose to do terrible things, and that if he did not, it was apt to be a proof that he was not able to do anything at all, and was therefore a bad king."[1]

Nevertheless, the heavy-handed barons did stop John, at least for the time being. In their eyes, John's chief offense had been the burdensome taxation he imposed to finance his war in France. John's signing of Magna Carta meant that he and his successors would find it very difficult to squeeze more money out of feudal barons. It became necessary for the Crown to turn elsewhere for revenue. Whither might kings turn? Why, to the knights (later called squires and country gentlemen) and to the burgesses (the merchants and the masters of the craft guilds).

In the latter half of the eighteenth century, and indeed early in the nineteenth century, it was common to declare that somehow Magna Carta was the beginning of representative government in England. No reputable historian in the closing decade of the twentieth century would so contend. Still—John's successors on the throne found it necessary, after the assembly at Runnymede, to seek better sources of revenue. And if the knights and the burgesses were asked by the kings to grant them money—well, those prosperous folk of the countryside and the towns must be summoned together so that the king's needs might be explained to them. In that sense, after some elapse of time, Magna Carta did help to bring about the royal summoning of representatives of the commons—the beginnings of the House of Commons, the first powerful representative assembly.

So England's kings turned to the class called "the commons"—this term meaning not the peasantry and the town laborers, but instead the sons of barons, the knights, the burgesses, certain small landowners— men of substance and knowledge. In the year 1242, King Henry III issued a writ directing the sheriff of each county to send, for consultation with the King's Council, "two good and discreet Knights of the Shire, whom the men of the country have chosen for this purpose in the stead of each and all of them, to consider along with the knights of other shires what aid they will give the king." (The choosing of jurymen already had given the English people some considerable experience in selecting representatives.) It was as *representatives* of the commons, speaking for the commons of their respective shires, that these knights went to confer with the king and his servants.

By 1295, when Edward I summoned a parliament (as usual in search of funds to conduct "the defense of the realm"), his writ was directed to "representatives of the counties and boroughs. " (This was the first formal employment of the word *representatives*.) Through qualified representatives, the commons were being admitted to some voice in affairs of state.[2] The writs sent out to summon Edward I's "Model Parliament" contained the phrase *quod omnes langit ab omnibus approbetur*—that is, "What concerns all, should be approved by all," a principle drawn from Roman jurisprudence. Additional taxation, in 1295, concerned all; therefore it was necessary to secure the assent of those substantial—and increasingly powerful—bodies of subjects and taxpayers classified as knights of the shire and burgesses of the towns.

It is not practicable here to run through the long history of the rise of "The Mother of Parliaments," the parliament of England, which in time came to meet frequently at Westminster, near London. Just now, it needs to be emphasized that representative government grew up in England—and to some degree, in other European states—as a means to persuade the commons to provide the government with regular sources of revenue. In England, the House of Commons came to hold "the power of the purse," the ability to grant or to deny funds requested by the king's ministers. Similarly, after 1789, in the United States, the House of Representatives, the "popular" house of Congress, alone was granted by the new Constitution the power to introduce "money bills" for federal expenditure.

From the end of the thirteenth century onward, the powers of Parliament, and of the House of Commons particularly, gradually grew. Lacking funds, the king could not even pay his troops; so the power of the purse became very real indeed. Yet this was a negative power merely: the Parliament was not permitted during the thirteenth and fourteenth centuries to initiate any legislation; that would come later. When Henry IV, in 1399, took the throne by force from Richard II, Parliament assented but declared its power to unmake and to enthrone kings for good cause. By the end of the Middle Ages, Parliament was not supreme in England, but representative government was well entrenched.

We must hasten on, in our pursuit of full representative government, to the seventeenth century—when, while the English were peopling the eastern seaboard of North America and contesting with France the mastery of that continent, civil wars convulsed Britain. When William of Orange and his consort Mary (daughter of the reigning James II) invaded England at the head of Dutch troops, Parliament formally dethroned James and enthroned in his stead William and Mary, in 1688-89. This was a great triumph for representative government, as fulfilling the will of the commons; for James, a Roman Catholic, had become desperately unpopular with the Protestant English. Yet the monarchy itself was not much shaken; William III, a strong king, did not permit Parliament to deprive the throne of its strength and dignity.

But Parliament, in 1689, presented William and Mary with the Bill of Rights, which, when accepted, in effect established the supremacy of Parliament. Out of that would grow the cabinet system of government. The Bill firmly endorsed representative government, sheltering it from forcible intervention by the king. (The electoral franchise, the right to vote, remained restricted to a minority of the English people, however: representative government and democracy are not necessarily synonymous.) And the English Bill of Rights would establish precedent for the American Bill of Rights that would be appended to the Constitution of the United States in 1791.

Meanwhile, seventeenth-century North America already was practicing representative government. What with struggles for power at home, successive British governments' American policies had been merely what Edmund Burke later would call "salutary neglect." The colonial governments all developed representative institutions on the British model—the only model that most of the colonists knew.

Self-Government in the Colonies before Independence

Only a dozen years after the first permanent English settlement was founded in Virginia, the colony's governor summoned a representative assembly, made up of twenty-two burgesses from eleven settlements; they met in the church at Jamestown. So began Virginia's House of Burgesses, the popular branch of that colony's legislature. A representative assembly for Massachusetts was formed in 1634; and eventually all thirteen mainland colonies, Georgia the last of them, obtained such assemblies.

Although three types of colonies stretched from Massachusetts and New Hampshire down to Georgia—chartered, royal, and proprietary colonies—a general pattern of government existed within each of them.* The principal executive was the governor, chosen in most colonies either by the king or by the colony's proprietor (with royal assent). He needed the support of the Council of colonial notables—in some colonies elected, in others appointed, in some instances chosen by a combination of those methods. This was the smaller legislative body. Presently governor and council were overshadowed by the colony's general assembly (under various titles), popularly elected. (By the latter decades of the seventeenth century, the colonies had a franchise more democratic than England's, though varying from colony to colony— most white male householders, over twenty-one years of age and possessed of substantial property, being granted the vote.) Marcus Wilson Jernegan succinctly describes the rivalry that promptly developed between governor and council on the one hand, and general assembly on the other:

> On the one side were the governor and council and other officials appointed by the King and governor. The governor was the mouthpiece of, and responsible to, the King; derived authority from the King; was conservative, and often looked on the colonies as a minor part of the British empire, which ought to subordinate its interests to those of the empire as a whole. In some cases the councils supported the governors in their views.

> On the other side stood the popular assembly, the mouthpiece of the people, deriving its authority from the people, tending towards radicalism, looking on the colony as more important than the empire, and pretending more and more to powers similar to those of the House of Commons. To make this system work harmoniously was like trying to mix oil and water.[3]

The several colonial assemblies, like the House of Commons, held the power of the purse: the assembly, not the council, initiated all money bills and could refuse to accept taxation within the colony. (Until 1765, Britain made no attempt to tax the North American colonies; but those colonies were expected to provide for their own public expenditures.) In most of the colonies, the governor was dependent upon the assembly for his salary: if he and the assembly disagreed

---

*Connecticut and Rhode Island, however, were wholly self-governing under their charters, and in Massachusetts the council was not appointed by the king.

overmuch, he would not be paid. The colonial assemblies maintained parliamentary agents in England: late in the colonial era, Benjamin Franklin was agent for Pennsylvania and other colonies, and Edmund Burke for the province of New York.[4]

During the British civil wars of the seventeenth century—fought in England, Scotland, Ireland, Wales, and overseas—the North American colonies were virtually independent of British direction. In Massachusetts and Virginia, on different occasions, the colonial governments set the government at Westminster at defiance. The several assemblies, towering more and more over the enfeebled authority of governor and council, enacted legislation much as they pleased, claiming that they were entitled to enjoy across the Atlantic all the chartered rights of Englishmen.[5]

Massachusetts was the most assertively free of the colonies. After only twenty years of existence, the colony of Massachusetts Bay with its capital at Boston, despite the settlers' Puritanism, virtually cut itself off from the Cromwellian "rule of the saints" in Britain. Charles M. Andrews writes,

> After 1650 the authorities at Boston avoided, as far as possible, all entanglements with English affairs, and resisted all attempts of Cromwell to interfere with their concerns. They refused to proclaim Richard Cromwell protector when ordered to do so, and at all times conducted themselves, to all intents and purposes, as a sovereign state. The general court of the colony levied taxes, provided for military defence, erected inferior corporations like that of Harvard College, regulated courts of justice, controlled the right of appeal, and assumed the highest prerogatives of sovereignty in coining money and hanging offenders, such as murderers, witches, and Quakers.[6]

In Massachusetts and New England generally, there prevailed what Edmund Burke was to call "the dissidence of dissent and the Protestantism of the Protestant religion." This spirit, hostile to Stuart king and Anglican bishop, found its expression in the colonial legislature and the Boston mob. In Massachusetts, during 1775, the passion for self-government would be expressed in rifle bullets.

Differing convictions about the British Constitution and its applicability to America eventually brought about the American Revolution, or War of Independence. In general British statesmen, both those of the Tory party and those of the Whig factions, thought of the thirteen colonies as lying under the authority of the Crown in Parliament, and so to be subordinate to the king's ministers and the statutes of Parliament. English public men assumed that the colonies' status in law was much like that of British cities and towns with their royal charters: municipal councils could adopt local ordinances and in general carry on local government, but only under authorization and approval by the Parliament; and so, they reasoned, it must be with those colonies across the Atlantic.

Except for Connecticut and Rhode Island, the colonial legislatures were required to submit for English approval or rejection whatever laws they might adopt. Parliament asserted its rightful power to legislate for the colonies as Parliament might find prudent. Until 1765, Parliament refrained from taxing the colonies directly, being more or less satisfied with the profits of trade with North America under the British Navigation Acts; but Parliament and the king's ministers held that they possessed the constitutional authority to tax America should they find it desirable to do so—quite as they were accustomed to govern and tax British municipalities.

The majority of leading men in the colonies, to the contrary, held that they were not wholly subject to the Parliament at Westminster. They acknowledged their ties to the British Crown, but maintained in effect that they possessed their own several parliaments—the colonial legislatures, dominated by the colonial assemblies. To those colonial legislatures the Americans sent representatives; they were permitted to send no representatives to the British Parliament at Westminster.

"No taxation without representation!" became the demand of the Patriots in America. That famous phrase is attributed to Daniel Gookin (1612-1687), an Irish-born Puritan soldier and magistrate, eminent in the affairs of Massachusetts. It had been a chief angry complaint of Parliament against King Charles I, in 1628, that the king had levied certain taxes without Parliament's consent. Charles reluctantly had accepted Parliament's Petition of Right, abandoning such taxes as a means to raise money for military operations; but the prolonged quarrel between King and Parliament would lead on to the terrible civil wars of the 1640s. Similarly, the American dispute over taxation would result in an American rising against the authority of King and Parliament, a lengthy destructive war, and separation of the thirteen colonies from the British Empire.

Matters did not come to a head, however, until 1765, when the

British ministry with no difficulty prevailed upon Parliament to pass the Stamp Act, intended to raise three hundred and fifty thousand pounds in the colonies, to pay in part for the cost of maintaining British troops there. This was "external taxation"—that is, taxation by the British Parliament, direct taxation without consent of the colonial legislatures, something unpleasantly new in the Thirteen Colonies. Now "No taxation without representation!" was shouted in the streets of American towns, and agents for the sale of revenue stamps stood in peril.

No peers having taken up residence in America, of course the colonies had no direct part in the House of Lords; nor had they ever been invited to elect members to the House of Commons. But the British argument was that although the King's American subjects were not "actually" represented in Parliament, still they were "virtually" represented. Such was the doctrine of Lord Mansfield (1705-1793), the most eminent British jurist of the eighteenth century, who contended that the Americans' interests were adequately protected and advanced by their British friends who sat in Parliament. It was not necessary to have the franchise in order to be politically represented. Although not elected by any formal constituency, the peers who sat in the House of Lords were conscientious, able representatives of all the English and Scots and Welsh and Irish country folk who happened to live anywhere in the vicinity of the great landed estates of those old families. A member of the House of Commons from Bolton or Old Sarum or Bristol or Malton—towns that varied greatly in size and population— represented not merely his local constituency but the people of the whole of Britain: he was concerned for the national interest; where he lived was incidental. (Now as then, many MP's do not live permanently, if at all, in the towns and counties where they were elected.) So ran the theory of virtual representation. Edmund Burke, friendly toward the American colonies though he was, found truth in the case for virtual representation. Most of the king's subjects in Great Britain did not possess the electoral franchise; but all the same, they had their representation in the House of Commons, sedulous for their interest and the national interest.

The American Patriots' demand was not really for literal representation in the Parliament at Westminster. How much good would that have done their cause? Even had each colony been authorized to send one or two members to the House of Commons, that American delegation would have been hopelessly outnumbered in the House by the members from England, Scotland, and Ireland. What the Americans meant by "no taxation without representation" was that they were to continue to be taxed only by their own colonial legislatures, in which they found themselves adequately represented already; they rejected all taxation, under any circumstances, imposed "externally" by Parliament.

Thus was representation hotly debated between the years 1765 and 1775; then came a tremendous explosion, "the shot heard 'round the world." Still, the British principle of representation would survive the Revolution and pass into both the general government and the several state governments of the United States of America. Before turning to that subject, we need to consider the nature and duties of a political representative, as expounded by a political "philosopher in action," Edmund Burke, in 1774 and 1780.

The Duties and Honor of a Representative

The Stamp Act turning out to be desperately unpopular on both sides of the Atlantic, and unenforceable in America, George III found it necessary to dismiss the Grenville ministry that had produced the Act, and to accept as his new prime minister the Marquis of Rockingham, the reforming leader of a powerful faction of the Whig party. Soon the Stamp Act was repealed by Parliament, although in its stead was adopted the Declaratory Act, affirming the abstract right of England to tax her colonies.

Rockingham brought with him into the new government as his private secretary—and soon-to-be member of the House of Commons—an Irishman of genius, Edmund Burke. Although the Rockingham ministry lasted little more than a year, by this advancement Burke was launched upon a political and literary career that still moves minds in both Britain and America.

On the floor of the House of Commons, Burke was the most eloquent and best-informed adversary of the endeavor of George III, as "Patriot King," to enlarge the power of the Crown both in Britain and in the colonies. He maintained that the North American colonials inherited "the chartered rights of Englishmen" and should not be dragooned into submission. For several years he was agent to the Court of Great Britain for the province of New York. He fought with all the strength that was in him to avert war between Britain and the thirteen colonies.

But it would be a confusion of ideas to say that Burke favored the American Revolution: he never favored any violent revolution. Believing as he did that history is "the known march of the ordinary providence of God," he sought peace, not upheaval; conciliation, not repression.

At the height of the American troubles, Burke was chosen by a majority of the electors of the city of Bristol to become one of their two members in the House of Commons. This was a considerable distinction, Bristol being the great port of the west and second among English towns only to London. On arriving there in November, 1774, after having won the poll, Burke informed the merchants and manufacturers and shipowners who had invited him to stand for the parliamentary seat that he meant to be their *representative*, not their delegate. Although constituents' wishes should have weight with their member in the House of Commons, Burke said, a representative is no mere delegate:

> His own unbiased opinion, his mature judgment, his enlightened conscience, he ought not to sacrifice to you, or to any set of men living. These he does not derive from your pleasure—no, nor from the law and the constitution. They are a trust from Providence, for the abuse of which he is deeply answerable. Your representative owes you, not his industry only, but his judgment, and he betrays, instead of serving you, if he sacrifices it to your opinion.[7]

Voters ought not to fancy, he continued, that they enjoy a right to issue authoritative instructions and mandates to their chosen representative. A member of Parliament sits there to secure the general good: "You chuse [*sic*] a member indeed; but when you have chosen him, he is not member of Bristol, but he is a member of *parliament*." Parliament is not a congress of ambassadors from towns and shires, in competition one with another for advantages; no, parliament "is a *deliberative* assembly of *one* nation, with *one* interest, that of the whole; where, not local purposes, not local prejudices ought to guide."[8]

The other Whig member of Parliament from Bristol, Cruger, somewhat slavishly promised the Bristol electors to obey to the letter their every instruction. Burke was too intelligent and too honest to make such professions. He had been elected, although by no great margin; during the next three years he behaved in the House of Commons as a true statesman should, pursuing a number of good ends, among them an endeavor to relieve Irish Catholics of the heavy civil disabilities under which they labored.

That was held against him in Bristol, where anti-Catholic feeling was strong. On some other questions, too, he lost support in commercial Bristol. In the general election of 1780 Burke had to campaign for reelection; he found that he had a hard row to hoe. As Carl Cone writes,

> Since 1774 he had been continually aware, and his friends had often reminded him, that his words and actions were carefully attended to by his constituents. He had refused to be servile, and when he supported measures the Bristol merchants disliked, he knew he was giving aid to his opponents. He had labored hard to do what he thought best for the nation and for Bristol; he had moved busily among government offices seeking favors and running errands for his constituents. These personal services, numerous and vexatious in wartime, were forgotten by Bristol in its displeasure over his conduct in large matters.[9]

After a few weeks of canvassing in Bristol, Burke came to understand that he could not win; and on 9 September 1780, he declined the election. Three days earlier, in an address to the Guildhall, he had defended his parliamentary conduct: "I come before you with the plain confidence of an honest servant in the equity of a candid and discerning master. I come to claim your approbation, not to amuse you with vain apologies, or with professions still more vain and senseless. I have lived too long to be served by apologies, or to stand in need of them."[10]

He had reminded the people of Bristol that electors ought to treat their political representatives with respect—lest they leave office in disgust, to be supplanted by rogues. "Let me say with plainness . . . that if by a fair, by an indulgent, by a gentlemanly behaviour to our representatives, we do not give confidence to their minds, and a liberal scope to their understandings; if we do not permit out members to act upon a *very* enlarged view of things; we shall at length infallibly degrade our national representation into a confused and scuffling bustle of local agency."[11]

This was taking high ground—higher than the electors of Bristol would tolerate. For what years remained to him in the House of Commons, Burke sat for the little borough of Malton, in Yorkshire, in which seat his friend the Marquis of Rockingham installed him.

Such sagacious eloquence as Burke uttered at Bristol is not heard today in Parliament nor in the Congress of the United States. Nor does one encounter many public persons, either side of the Atlantic, who meet Burke's norms of integrity and ability for political representatives. "Gentlemen, we must not be peevish with those who serve the people," Burke had told his Guildhall audience. It never has been easy to find out men and women at once able and willing to be active in representative government—to serve not out of ambition merely, or desire for power, but from concern for the common good. The dour or jeering faces Burke encountered in the streets of Bristol, as he canvassed for votes in 1780, are to be seen still in every political contest more than two centuries later. "What have you done for me *lately*?" the constituent inquires, now as then.[12]

At the very time when Burke was demanding that Lord North's ministry should let the Americans govern themselves through their colonial legislatures, Virginia's House of Burgesses and some other colonial assemblies were dominated by gentlemen who were true representatives, fully meeting Burke's standards. Many of them were planters of old families, self-assured and independent of judgment. Daniel Boorstin describes them:

> This security of social position bred a wholesome vigor of judgment which made the Virginia House of Burgesses a place for deliberation and discussion rarely found among modern legislatures. Burgesses came close to Edmund Burke's ideal of the representative who owed allegiance not to the whim of his consistency but only to his private judgment. The voters in colonial Virginia had just enough power to prevent the irresponsibility of their representatives, but not enough to secure their servility. This was a delicate balance, but it had a great deal to do with the effectiveness of the legislature. . . . The most famous example of this Burkean independence comes from a later year: in 1788, in the Virginian Convention called to ratify the new Federal Constitution, at least eight delegates voted for the new government against the wishes of their electors. . . . In those days it was still customary (at least in Virginia) to give more time to the deliberations of his House than to answering his mail from constituents, to making "news" in legislative committees, or to seeking jobs for faithful supporters. American folklore has only a little exaggerated: the Virginia House of Burgesses was a meeting of gods on Olympus compared to a modern state legislature.[13]

Modern legislatures, even in America and Britain, do not closely resemble either the House of Commons in Edmund Burke's day or the

House of Burgesses in Patrick Henry's day. Yet Burke's words at Bristol, not forgotten altogether in Britain or America, ever since have reminded some thinking and conscientious men and women of democracy's need for an honorable aristocracy of high talents that may redeem representative government from mediocrity and error. Seven years after Burke declined the Bristol poll, there assembled at Philadelphia some fifty-five American gentlemen, experienced in practical politics and well informed concerning British political institutions and political thought, most of whom were qualified, in knowledge as in character, to represent their constituents of the new Thirteen States. The Constitutional Convention of 1787, indeed, was an achievement of representative government that never has been excelled.

Representation on a Grand Scale

Representative government on a scale so vast as the United States of America never had been conceived of before. To the Parliament at Westminster had come only members from England, Scotland, and Wales; Ireland then had its own parliament at Dublin. In 1787, the principal states of the European continent had no representative assemblies at all; and when the Old Regime in France and other countries would collapse, a few years later, the National Assembly, the Convention, and other revolutionary assemblies would be things of terror.

An obvious reason why the Americans succeeded in their experiment with national representative government, in contrast with the ghastly failures of Europe within the following decade, is that the English settlers had carried on their own representative governments for a century and a half. During the era of "salutary neglect," when the Stuarts, Cromwell, and Parliament had been preoccupied by troubles closer to London, the people of the thirteen colonies had learned the arts of self-governance. Besides, the leaders of the new Republic, read in Blackstone's *Commentaries* and Hume's *History of England*—and some of them schooled in England—apprehended very well the story of the growth of Parliament from the thirteenth century to the eighteenth. To the citizens of the United States, even those little schooled, representative government was no new mysterious undertaking. By and large, that pattern of politics had served them well.

Thus, during the Revolution, it had been fairly easy to convert the thirteen colonial governments into similar state governments. Connecticut and Rhode Island simply made their seventeenth-century colonial charters into their state constitutions, striking out references to the king. In the other new states, some tinkering with political institutions occurred during the way years (Pennsylvania first adopting a radical constitution, to supplant it with a moderate constitution in 1790)—yet by the beginning of the last decade of the eighteenth century, all state constitutions had settled into a fairly common pattern. This was the conservative political system described by John Fiske in his famous volume *The Critical Period of American History*:

> Thus the various state governments were repetitions on a small scale of what was then supposed to be the triplex government of England, with its Kings, Lords, and Commons. The governor answered to the king with his dignity curtailed by election for a short period, and by narrowly limited prerogatives. The senate answered to the House of Lords, except in being a representative and not a hereditary body. It was supposed to represent more especially that part of the community which was possessed of most wealth and consideration; and in several states the senators were apportioned with some reference to the amount of taxes paid by different parts of the state. The senate of New York, in direct imitation of the House of Lords, was made a supreme court of errors. On the other hand, the assembly answered to the House of Commons, save that its power was really limited by the senate as the House of Commons is not really limited by the House of Lords.[14]

That general pattern of state governments survives to the present day, even though all state constitutions, over the years, have been much amended and often have given way to fresh constitutions—not radically different in most matters from their predecessors. That pattern is English—but based upon English parliamentary (national) government, not upon the government of English counties. By the time General Cornwallis had surrendered at Yorktown, the royal governors were jailed or fled, their chairs occupied by state governors; the governors' councils had given way to state senates; and the various venerable colonial assemblies had been restyled houses of representatives—except for Virginia, where the House of Burgesses retained its honorable old name, and North Carolina, which called its lower house the House of Commons. In substance, however—and even in property qualifications for holding public office and for voting—representative government in the new republic had suffered no rash innovation. America's state governments of the formative era, in short, all were British or British-colonial in character; and even today, with one or two exceptions, the governments of the fifty states are British-modelled.

Building a national representative system was another matter: the file afforded no precedent for such an undertaking, except for the British experience; and the British political system was centralized, a condition that few Americans desired, and that anyway would have been impracticable in sprawling North America. Yet the remarkable talents of those fifty-five delegates at Philadelphia surmounted the difficulty—after a series of expedient and prudent compromises.

The federal system of government devised at the Constitutional Convention in 1787 is America's principal contribution to modern political institutions. It was original, for nothing much resembling federalism (to use the term in the modern sense) had existed previously in the world. It began as a compromise between those delegates who desired a very strong general (or even centralized) government, and those delegates who desired to preserve the sovereignty of the several states. As matters worked out, the federal system divided between the general government and the state governments certain political responsibilities. Later this device would be emulated in several European and Latin American countries, for it reconciled the need for national defense and an integrated economy with the need for state (or provincial) self-government. Alexis de Tocqueville, in the 1830s, would perceive the originality and the wisdom of America's unique federalism.[15]

Thus the new United States developed a scheme of dual representation: the people, in their national capacity, sending political representatives to Washington (which supplanted Philadelphia and New York as national capital); the people, in their capacity as citizens of a particular state, sending political representatives to their state capital. By and large, this plan of representation has worked well during two centuries.

Although representation within the fifty states is very much on the British model, then, the federal structure of the United States owes little to British experience or theory. Yet within America's general government itself—in the House of Representatives, in the Senate, and after a fashion in the office of the Presidency—one readily recognizes English institutions as a source.

The federal House of Representatives, as its powers and functions are specified in Article I of the Constitution, much resembles the

House of Commons—but the Commons as that House was about the time of the American Revolution, not as the House of Commons stands near the end of the twentieth century. (Nowadays the House of Commons is far more powerful—nay, almost omnipotent—within the United Kingdom; while the House of Representatives' share of federal authority is much what it was two centuries ago.) Money bills must originate with the House of Representatives, as with the House of Commons; and the former, like the latter, can be called "the popular house" of Congress, because its members serve for terms of two years merely, and therefore must stand for election more frequently.

Sir Henry Maine, the great English historical jurist, emphasizes the British origin of the popular house of Congress:

> The House of Representatives . . . is unquestionably a reproduction of the House of Commons. No Constitution but the British could have suggested section 7 of Article I of the Federal Constitution, which lays down a British principle, and settles a dispute which had arisen upon it in a particular way. "All Bills raising Revenue shall originate in a House of Representatives; but the Senate may propose or concur with amendments as in other Bills." . . . The House of Representatives is a much more exclusively legislative body than either the Senate of the United States or than the present British House of Commons.[16]

At the time of the framing of the American Constitution, the British Parliament was still chiefly "a body of critics" rather than two houses of legislators; the cabinet system, by which a committee of the dominant party in the House of Commons forms and directs the sovereign's government, had not yet fully developed. The cabinet system cannot develop under the American Constitution; therefore the House of Representatives is far less powerful than the House of Commons. But in 1787, the Framers at Philadelphia intended to emulate the House of Commons closely.

The United States Senate roughly parallels the House of Lords, and was intended to provide a strong check upon the House of Representatives—as the Lords checked the Commons, and to a limited extent do so still. There being no peerage in America, the Senate necessarily was an elective, not an hereditary, body; but dignity was conferred upon the senators by there being only two from each state; by a six-year term of office; by a higher age requirement; and by powers, not possessed by the House, relative to the executive branch of the federal government. The Senate was assigned by the Constitution the power of trying presidents of the United States, they having been impeached by the House; of confirming or rejecting the presidential nomination of candidates for certain high offices in the government; and of restraining the President's treaty-making power by the constitutional provision, in Article II, Section 2, that the President must obtain "advice and consent" from the Senate.

Until ratification of the seventeenth amendment to the Constitution, in 1913, United States senators were elected by their state legislatures, not by popular vote. (Since that change, in general the abilities of United States senators have diminished, Eugene McCarthy remarks—in part because a statewide constituency, often of millions of voters, places great burdens upon senators from the more populous states, who find themselves compelled to travel frequently about the whole state, courting voters, and neglecting the business of the Senate accordingly.) Also, until 1913, most state legislatures tended usually to choose distinguished men, natural aristocrats of the breed of Daniel Webster and John C. Calhoun, to represent their state, to that state's honor and advantage; while democratic electorates are less discriminating usually. Although the standards in debate, breeding, and integrity of the Senate never have equalled those of the House of Lords (which has been called the grandest debating society in the world), still the Senate (today far more powerful than the House of Lords) functions effectually, much of the time, as a prudent Second Chamber.

Even the American Presidency is a representative institution, in one aspect, derived from British example. For the president of the United States is an elected king. The Constitution's Framers understood the necessity for a powerful executive for the nation; and so they conferred upon the presidential office almost precisely the powers enjoyed by King George III not long before 1765, during the happy time of the "salutary neglect" of the colonies by the British government. (The Framers, many of whom had hotly denounced George III at one time or another, did not inform the public that they were taking that King as their model executive; yet clearly they had his office in mind.)

"On the face of the Constitution of the United States," Henry Maine comments,

the resemblance of the President of the United States to the European King, and especially to the King of Great Britain, is too obvious for mistake. The President has, in various degrees, a number of powers which those who know something of Kingship in its general history recognize at once as peculiarly associated with it and with no other institution. The whole Executive power is vested in him. He is Commander-in-Chief of the Army and Navy. He makes treaties with the advice and consent of the Senate, and with the same advice and consent he appoints Ambassadors, Ministers, Judges, and all high functionaries. He has a qualified veto on legislation. He convenes Congress, when no special time of meeting has been fixed. It is conceded in the *Federalist* that the similarity of the new President's office to the functions of the British King was one of the points on which the opponents of the Constitution fastened.[17]

True, the kingly president obtains his high office by election, not inheritance; true, he is elected at first for a term of four years merely; true, there are restraints upon his power. But some European kings, notably in Poland, were elected; and restraints existed upon the powers of George III and other monarchs, too.

It is tolerably clear, Maine continues,

that the mental operation through which the framers of the America Constitution passed was this: they took the King of Great Britain, went through his powers, and restrained them whenever they appeared to be excessive or unsuited to the circumstances of the United States. It is remarkable that the figure they had before them was not a generalized English king nor an abstract Constitutional monarch; it was no anticipation of Queen Victoria, but George III himself whom they took for their model.[18]

The powers of George III about 1765 were very much greater than those possessed by Queen Elizabeth II today. For the strong cabinet system, advocated by Edmund Burke and his friends, was only in early process of development about 1765; nowadays, as suggested earlier in this chapter, Britain is governed in fact by a committee of the House of Commons, called the cabinet. The powers of the American president, on the contrary, are a good deal greater now than they were at the end of the eighteenth century—although no constitutional amendment has authorized that enlargement. And the president, unlike the British sovereign, is restrained by no cabinet originating in the popular house of the legislature.

Why are we to regard the president of the United States as bound up with political representation, inherited from Britain? Because the president is elected, every four years, by a vote of the whole nation, polled state by state, and nominally decided by the electoral college, but actually a popular vote. So far as anybody in America may be said to represent the people's general will, it is the president: television, radio, and the newspapers exalt presidential candidates in the public's eye, so that most voters know more about those presidential aspirants, and about the incumbent President, than they know about their state senators and representatives, or their senators and representatives in the Congress. This concentration on the presidential office raises the danger of "plebiscitary democracy," in which the public comes to prefer a government of men over a government of laws: but be that as it may, some of the "divinity that doth hedge a king" seems to envelop, in many citizens' eyes, the person of the president.

Although their "actual" political representatives at Washington are senators and congressmen, many Americans pay more heed to the presidential figure who seems to them their "virtual" representative. (That English term "virtual representation" was anathema to Thomas Jefferson.)

Discussing parliamentary representation for Irish Catholics in 1792, Edmund Burke wrote to Sir Hercules Langrishe, M. P., about types of political representation. He was indignant that Catholics had obtained neither actual nor virtual representation in their own country.

"Virtual representation," Burke declared,

is that in which there is a communion of interests, and a sympathy in feelings and desires between those who act in the name of any description of people, and the people in whose name they act, though not actually chosen by them. This is virtual representation. Such a representation I think to be, in many cases, even better than the actual. It possesses most of its advantages, and is free from many of its inconveniences; it corrects the irregularities in the literal representation, when the shifting current of human affairs, or the acting of public interests in different ways, carry it obliquely from its first line of direction. The people may err in their choice; but common interest and common sentiment are rarely mistaken.[19]

In the United States, virtual representation is not unknown today—although the Revolution was fought to secure for Americans actual representation. (Edmund Burke had been their most earnest virtual representative in Parliament, until the battles of Lexington and Concord.)

For in one era or another, from the beginning of the Republic, millions of American citizens have thought of the president of the United States—Washington, or Lincoln, or Cleveland, or Theodore Roosevelt, or Franklin Roosevelt, or Reagan—as their virtual representative: their kindly and somewhat kingly protector of their rights and interests, in this naughty world. That sentiment of attachment to some grand political figure, that yearning for a powerful tribune-representative, also is an inheritance from Britain. (Walter Bagehot called the English "a deferential people.")

Tories, at least, looked upon King George III, throughout his long reign, as their virtual representative, trusting him more than they did the Whig-dominated Parliament. The older and madder the King grew, the more he was loved by the people. Burke, who had heaped oratorical coals of fire upon the King's head in the 1760s and 1770s, praised him most highly in 1790.[20]

Similarly, Americans' hostility toward Britain faded away after the end of the War of 1812. Today both countries are constitutional representative democracies; and both are more stable politically than are any other political systems of major countries near the end of the twentieth century.

Notes

1. Rebecca West, *The Court and the Castle* (London: Macmillan, 1958), 35.
2. The entire text of Magna Carta may be found in Carl Stephenson's and Frederick George Marcham's *Sources of English Constitutional History: A Selection of Documents from A. D. 600 to the Present* (New York: Harper & Brothers, 1937) and similar manuals. A long-standard collection of medieval English documents, in Latin, annotated, is Bishop William Stubbs' *Select Charters and Other Illustrations . . . to the Reign of Edward the First* (Oxford: Clarendon Press, ninth edition, with corrections, 1946). A thorough recent book that takes up the beginnings of representation in England is Ronald Butt's *A History of Parliament: The Middle Ages* (London: Constable, 1989); see especially chapter 2, "Henry III: the Emergence of Parliament."
3. Marcus Wilson Jernegan, *The American Colonies, 1492-1750: A Study of Their Political, Economic and Social Development* (New York: Frederick Ungar, 1965), 276–77.
4. For Franklin as colonial agent in London, see, for instance, Carl van Doren, *Benjamin Franklin* (New York: Viking Press, 1938), chapter 15; for Burke, see Ross J. S. Hoffman, *Edmund Burke, New York Agent* (Philadelphia: American Philosophical Society, 1956).
5. Two standard works on the colonies are Charles McLean Andrews' *The Colonial Period* (New York: Henry Holt, 1912) and Lyon G. Tyler's *England in America* (1904) (reprint, New York: Cooper Square Publishers, 1968). Of course much diversity in political institutions existed, from colony to colony. For Virginia, see Charles S. Sydnor, *Gentlemen Freeholders: Political Practices in Washington's Virginia* (Chapel Hill: University of North Carolina Press, 1952).

6. Charles McLean Andrews, *Colonial Self-Government, 1652-1689* (New York: Harper & Brothers, 1905), 44–45.
7. Edmund Burke, "Speech to the Electors of Bristol, on his being declared . . . duly elected . . .", November 3, 1774, in *The Works of the Right Honourable Edmund Burke* (London: C. and J. Rivington, 1826), vol. III, 18–19.
8. Ibid., 20.
9. Carl B. Cone, *Burke and the Nature of Politics: The Age of the American Revolution* (Lexington: University of Kentucky Press, 1957), 384. See also G. E. Weare, *Edmund Burke's Connection with Bristol, from 1774 till 1780* (Bristol: William Bennett, 1844).
10. Burke (1826), *Works*, vol. III, 356.
11. Ibid., vol. III, 360.
12. Among recent biographies of Burke are Stanley Ayling's *Edmund Burke: His Life and Opinions* (New York: St. Martin's Press, 1988) and Russell Kirk's *Edmund Burke: a Genius Reconsidered* (second edition, Peru, Ill.: Sherwood Sugden, 1988). A collection of twenty-one critical essays on Burke by various hands, edited by Daniel E. Ritchie, is *Edmund Burke: Appraisals and Applications* (New Brunswick, N. J.: Transaction Publishers, 1990). Peter J. Stanlis' essays on Burke are collected in his volume *Edmund Burke: the Enlightenment and Revolution* (New Brunswick, N. J.: Transaction Publishers, 1991).
13. Daniel Boorstin, *The Americans: The Colonial Experience* (New York: Random House, 1958), 118–19.
14. John Fiske, *The Colonial Period of American History, 1783-1789)* (Boston: Houghton Mifflin, 1891), 68.
15. For several serious essays on federalism, see *A Nation of States*, edited by Robert Goldwin (Chicago: Rand McNally, 1963).
16. Sir Henry Maine, *Popular Government* (1885) (Indianapolis: Liberty Classics, 1970), 228–29.
17. Ibid., 212.
18. Ibid., 213.
19. Edmund Burke, *A Letter to Sir H. Langrische, Bart., M. P., on the Subject of the Roman Catholics of Ireland, and the Propriety of Admitting Them to the Principles of the Constitution*, in Burke, *Works*, vol. VI, 260.
20. For the stubborn and courageous political conduct of George III during the later stages of the war in America, see Sir Herbert Butterfield, *George III, Lord North, and the People* (London: G. Bell and Sons, 1949).

5

Mores and Minds

The Habits of the Heart

In the year 1775, when the War of Independence began, the thirteen colonies had a population of perhaps 2,418,000 people, of whom possibly one-fifth were black.[1] Small Dutch, German, and Swedish minorities were included in these statistics, but the vast majority of white inhabitants were of British stock: Englishmen, Scots, Northern Irish, and Welsh. Their *mores*—that is, their moral habits and beliefs, their social customs, their intellectual inclinations, their prejudices (good or bad)—were British in origin. Those moral traditions and habits and manners still strongly influence the nearly 260,000,000 people who live in the United States nowadays.

By 1790, there were some 3,929,000 Americans (3,172,000 white, 757,000 black) according to the first national census. Huge waves of immigration from Germany, Ireland, eastern and southern Europe, and Asia would occur, caused by Old World poverty or by political disorder, during the next hundred years—beginning about the middle of the nineteenth century with the hungry southern Irish (chiefly Catholics) and the Germans in the late 1840s and the 1850s, and the first wave of Chinese to California about the same time. Two centuries after the first United States census was taken, nearly every race and nationality in the world had contributed to the American population, but the culture of America remains British. (Descendants of English-speaking settlers in the United States are less numerous today than descendants of German-speaking ancestors, yet America's culture has not been greatly altered by a century and a half of German immigration.) The many millions of newcomers to the United States have accepted integration into the British-descended American culture with little protest, and often with great willingness.

Alexis de Tocqueville—whose study of the American democracy was the greatest sociological work of the nineteenth century—wandering about the United States during 1831-32, found the American Republic a success, for the most part; thus unlike other democracies, ancient or modern, they soon having gone down to ruin. A great gulf separated the violently unstable republics of Latin America from the stable and prospering society of the United States. What was the cause of this superiority? So Tocqueville inquired of himself.

Might it be the circumstances—the geographical situation of the United States, the natural resources, equality of social conditions? No, South America and French Canada possessed circumstances as favorable, but had not achieved similar happy results.

Might it be America's laws? Those laws were more significant, indeed, than the circumstances; but although most American laws contributed to social happiness, some of those laws were dangerous, and the emulation of those laws by Mexico had not prospered.

Might it be the mores (*moeurs*) of the people of the United States? (Tocqueville used that word "mores," since very fashionable among sociologists, "to cover the whole moral and intellectual state of a people . . . to cover the sum of the moral and intellectual dispositions of man in society.") He found the ways of the American West very difficult from those of America's East. Why was government in the East strong and orderly, while in the West "the powers of society seem to proceed at random"?

Deciding that the difference lay in the mores, the moral habits and customs, the modes of thought, the manners (in the larger sense of that last word), Tocqueville concluded that "It is their mores, then, that make the Americans of the United States, alone among Americans, capable of maintaining the rule of democracy; and it is mores again that makes the various Anglo-American democracies more or less orderly and prosperous. . . . The importance of mores is a universal truth to which study and experience continually bring us back. I find it occupies the central position in my thoughts; all my ideas come back to it in the end."[2]

In every culture of the past, everywhere in the world, the principal source of a culture's mores—its traditional customs, its way of regarding the human condition, its principles of morality—has been religious belief. This has been true even when many people within that culture have ceased to feel any devotion to the old religious creed; even so, habit and custom fix them in a routine of existence, so that men may open doors for ladies even though they have forsworn the traditions of civility; boys may refrain from pilfering because "Dad taught me not to" even though they never attended Sunday school; and women may be most charitable even though they have forgotten the Golden Rule and the injunctions of Saint Paul. Thus a vestigial and peripheral morality may survive the withering of the cult from which a culture arose originally.

Be that as it may, in eighteenth-century America the Christian religion was quick enough, if somewhat attentuated in the western wilds when Tocqueville and his colleague Beaumont made their way through the forests and swamps of Michigan. The first British colony had been planted at Jamestown, by Anglican adventurers, so that Virginia grew up as territory of the Church of England. Thirteen years later, the Pilgrims had settled at Plymouth, devout dissenters. The Puritans had begun to build Boston in 1630, and Calvinist churches or their more radical offshoots had triumphed throughout New England.

Pilgrims and Puritans, and Lord Baltimore's Catholics who settled in Maryland in 1634, all were dissenters from the Church of England. So were William Penn's Quakers, who established themselves in Pennsylvania and New Jersey in 1682. The thousands of Scots and Ulstermen, Calvinists of another species, sons and daughters of the Kirk of Scotland, began to pour out to the frontiers of the colonies, in the West, so early as 1715; they too did not subscribe to the Thirty-Nine Articles of the Church of England; nor did the Baptists, who began to grow in numbers in the colonies about the middle of the eighteenth century. Less bitter in their dissent were John Wesley's Methodists, very busy and numerous toward the end of the century. (Wesley always regarded himself as an Anglican—but with a different method.)

A congeries of sects, these, that had broken with the Church by law established in England. Were they in conformity to the mores of old England? Yes, for all professed their Christian faith, all read King James's Bible (with the exception of the Catholics, who had the Douay Bible); all preached the theological virtues of faith, hope, and charity. All spoke and read English, all lived under English law, all abided by many old English prescriptions and usages. Theirs was Christianity in British forms.

True, their religion, long before, had come from Jerusalem by way of Rome; it had not sprung up prophetically at Canterbury. Nevertheless, the people of British North America had learned their Christian doctrine from British lips and British pens. Whatever their theological differences, they all were reared in a British climate of opinion, with the Ten Commandments at the back of their minds, when not in the forefront. The Anglicans among them—the most numerous of the denominations in America—had been accustomed since infancy to the noble Anglican liturgy and presently to the Book of Common Prayer. (A large proportion of the colonial leaders were communicants of the Church of England; of the fifty-five delegates to the Constitutional Convention in 1787, some twenty-eight or twenty-nine were Episcopalians—that is, Anglicans.)

In short, American Christianity was British Christianity, of whatever persuasion, transplanted. Mores and morals flowing from religious doctrine, the colonials' morality and folkways were the products of British culture. Among the delegates to the Constitutional Convention were one Lutheran; one (or possibly two) members of the Dutch Reformed Church; and merely one or two Deists (English variety, though). Saint Augustine of Canterbury might have rejoiced at his ascendancy in the New World, all others being sheep of his flock.[3]

Tocqueville perceived that this widespread religious belief—or, in some, this outward profession of belief—gave the American democracy its strength and its temperateness. "There is an innumerable multitude of sects in the United States. They are all different in the worship they offer to the creator, but all agree concerning the duties of man to one another. Each sect worships God in its own fashion, but all preach the same morality in the name of God." Some men follow their habits rather than their convictions, no doubt—for we cannot know the heart—but "Nonetheless, America is still the place where the Christian religions has kept the greatest power over men's minds."

Out of Christian teaching arose America's mores. "I do not doubt for an instant," Tocqueville continued,

> that the great severity of mores which one notices in the United States has its primary origin in beliefs. There religion is often powerless to restrain men in the midst of innumerable temptations which fortune offers. It cannot moderate their

eagerness to enrich themselves, which everything contributes to arouse, but it reigns supreme in the souls of the women, and it is women who shape mores. Certainly of all countries in the world America is the one in which the marriage tie is most respected and where the highest and truest conception of conjugal happiness has been conceived.

In Europe almost all the disorders of society are born around the domestic hearth and not far from the nuptial bed. It is there that men come to feel scorn for natural ties and legitimate pleasures and develop a taste for disorder, restlessness of spirit, and instability of desires. Shaken by the tumultuous passions which have often troubled his own house, the European finds it hard to submit to the authority of the state's legislators. When the American returns from the turmoil of politics to the bosom of the family, he immediately finds a perfect picture of order and peace. There all his pleasures are simple and natural and his joys innocent and quiet, and as the regularity of life brings him happiness, he easily forms the habit of regulating his opinions as well as his tastes.[4]

By English and Scottish theologians, moralists, and preachers had Christian morals been imparted to the Americans, at some remove in time, from across the sea, and in a diversity of communions: by Richard Hooker, John Knox, Jeremy Taylor, John Bunyan, Sir Thomas Browne, George Fox, John Wesley, and more — all British. At the end of the colonial period, the skepticism and deism of the French Enlightenment would touch only a few Americans, Franklin and Jefferson eminent among them.

Marital fidelity and the integrity of the family aside, what moral habits and beliefs gave solidity and continuity to the American Republic? Tocqueville does not catalogue them; but any person familiar with biographies of leading Americans of Tocqueville's time or earlier, and who has some acquaintance with the journals and correspondence of thoughtful American men and women of yesteryear, may find it possible to compile a list of America's mores during the formative years of the Republic.[5]

One cultural trait common among the Americans was high courage in danger or adversity. These were a folk who had carved out civilization from the wilderness, fished profitably in wild seas, fought the Indians and the French and the Spaniards — and, latterly, the British and the Hessians. Cowardice was rare enough — in part because of society's vigorous contempt for that vice. No one was much surprised that the colonies' leading men would venture their lives, their fortunes, and their sacred honor in the cause of no taxation without representation—when, if they failed, the penalty was to be hanged by the neck until dead.

Another customary attitude was willingness to sacrifice in the present for future presumed good. This it was that moved pioneer men and women to labor all their lives cutting down forests, pulling the stumps, and ploughing the land for the first time—to benefit their children rather than themselves. (During the youth of this writer, in Michigan stumps still were being pulled and virgin land ploughed by toil-worn elderly farmers, for the sake of the rising generation.) Or, with John Adams, other Americans would say, "He who plants trees, plants generations." The Americans of Tocqueville's time held the conviction that "God helping, work prospers"—although only well-schooled Americans were aware that this precept was drawn from Vergil, Publius Vergilius Maro, the greatest of Latin poets.

Conspicuous among American mores was the strong inclination toward household independence: the isolated farmstead rather than the tight-knit village, an individualism extending all the way to Daniel Boone's determination to shift farther westward whenever neighbors came so near to him that he could hear their dog bark. This love of spaciousness was somewhat atoned for, however, by hospitable reception of most wayfarers and newcomers.

Shrewd practical intelligence was encountered frequently in America by European observers. In view of the motives of immigrants to British North America during the colonial era, this characteristic might have been expected. People who succeed in fleeing from great social disasters or grinding persecution commonly possess keen intellects—as witness the Vietnamese, Cambodians, and Laotians who have made their way to the United States, surmounting great suffering and hazard, during the 1970s and 1980s. So, too, was it with those black slaves before 1865, who succeeded in escaping from the Southern states to Canada. A large part of colonial America's population consisted of such strong and courageous fugitives, or their descendants, folk with their wits about them: Pilgrims, Puritans, Quakers, English Catholics, Huguenots, refugees. from the English Civil Wars of the seventeenth century (Cavaliers among them), Scots Highlanders (fled or "transported" after the failure of the Jacobite rising of 1745), and yet others.

Frequently this select native intelligence chose industrial and commercial occupations in America—the Du Pont family, in Delaware, being the most splendid example of such success—and in general Americans had habits of fair dealings and commercial efficiency. From England, so long great in international trade; from England, where the Industrial Revolution commenced about the middle of the eighteenth century—from the English, whom Napoleon called a nation of shopkeepers, came America's proficiency in commerce, industry, and banking, and America's early industrial technology.

As Henry Adams writes, describing the United States in the year 1800,

> The average American was more intelligent than the average European, and was becoming every year still more active-minded as the new movement of society caught him up and swept him through a life of more varied experiences. On all sides the national mind responded to its stimulants. Deficient as the American was in the machinery of higher instruction; remote, poor; unable by any exertion to acquire the training, the capital, or even the elementary text-books he needed for a fair development of his natural powers,—his native energy and ambition already responded to the spur applied to them. Some of his triumphs were famous throughout the world; for Benjamin Franklin had raised high the reputation of American printers, and the actual President of the United States, who signed with Franklin the treaty of peace with Great Britain, was the son of a small farmer, and had himself kept a school in his youth."* [6]

Tocqueville recognizes intellectual curiosity as associated with American mores. He emphasizes, too, Americans' respect for the laws. In the United States, he writes, "there is no numerous and perpetually turbulent crowd regarding the law as a natural enemy to fear and to suspect." [7] (That remark is less true in the present era than it was in Tocqueville's time.)

Having named among America's mores a general chastity within the family, courage, willingness to sacrifice, household independence, and shrewd practical intelligence—all these falling within Tocqueville's rather broad concept of mores—one might go on to describe yet others. But their name is legion. David Hackett Fischer, in his fat book *Albion's Seed: Four British Folkways in America* (1989), lists twenty-four "folkways" that will be found in any given culture, rang-

---

*John Adams

ing from speech ways through sex ways and death ways and learning ways, to freedom ways. Folkways being near akin to Tocqueville's mores, we cannot embark in this book upon an extended analysis of twenty-four or more American mores at the beginning of the nineteenth century.

These folkways, mores among them, brought to colonial America by four British migrations, still persist in the regions of the United States where those groups settled. Dr. Fischer examines the four chief shifts, in the seventeenth and eighteenth centuries, across the Atlantic: Puritans from East Anglia to Massachusetts; Cavaliers and indentured servants from the south of England to Virginia; Quakers from the North Midlands of England to the Delaware; and "Borderlands to the Backcountry" (Scots, Ulstermen, and northern English to the Appalachian backcountry, the Indian frontier). He proves exhaustively that despite large demographic and social changes, the folkways and mores of those several types of British colonists still may be discerned, and still influence everyday life, in the four distinct regions of America where they severally settled.

"Today less than twenty percent of the American population have any British ancestors at all," Mr. Fischer remarks. "But in a cultural sense most Americans are Albion's seed, no matter who their own forebears may have been. Strong echoes of four British folkways still may be heard in the major dialects of American speech, in the regional patterns of American life, and in the continuing conflict between four different ideas of freedom in the United States."[8]

The mores, derived from Britain, that Tocqueville discerned among Americans at the beginning of the 1830s, gave the American people a firm footing for their decisions and actions. They made possible the permanence of America's democratic republic. Rooted in centuries of human experience in Britain, supplemented by generations of life in North America, these mores were what Edmund Burke called "the wisdom of the species" and "the wisdom of our ancestors." In any difficult hour, these mores might provide guidance. They, too, constituted a patrimony.

British Learning in the New Nation

For a glimpse of the beginnings of higher education in America, one may visit the campus of the second oldest college of the country,

William and Mary, at Williamsburg, the colonial capital of Virginia. There students still throng in and out of the College's central building, with its handsome dome; Sir Christopher Wren, the architect of St. Paul's Cathedral and other grand London churches, is said to have designed that fine college building. Nearby is a humbler structure, the Brafferton, which was a school for Indians in the College's early days; and where visiting professors and lecturers at the College, this writer among them, still were lodged so late as the 1950s. On the lawn before the Wren Building stands an antique statue of Lord Botetourt, the royal governor of Virginia from 1768 to 1770.

The College of William and Mary is a very British foundation; and the traditions of civility cling to it. It was founded in 1693. Two hundred and seventy-five years later, alumni sponsored the casting of bronze commemorative medallions, one of which was presented to this writer. It bears the profiles of King William and Queen Mary, their noses strong, their look confident; the College had been chartered, with royal allowances for endowment, in the fourth year of their reign. In all the thirteen colonies, only Harvard College (established in 1636, when Massachusetts Bay colony had been in existence merely a half-dozen years) was older.

At this College of William and Mary, young Virginian men—not a great many of them—studied languages, theology, philosophy, mathematics, and the sciences. Its model was an English residential college, and its object was to rear up in Virginia a class of leaders, to whom some measure of wisdom and virtue—old Plato's ends of education—had been imparted. The College was expected to graduate gentlemen—American gentlemen, of course, but patterned upon the English idea and reality of a gentleman.

All nine colleges founded in British North America before the Revolution emulated, as best they could, the two English universities, Cambridge and Oxford. Princeton, a Presbyterian institution, had connections with the Scottish universities. No American college then ventured to style itself a university; but their curricula reflected that of the British universities. The study of Hebrew, Greek, and Latin loomed large, and so did theology. These nine colleges drew their support from colonial churches. Many of their graduates would be ordained clergymen upon graduation, and a surprising proportion of graduates, entering colonial politics, rose to public office. The collegiate study of rhetoric—"the art of persuasion, beautiful and just"—fitted young men for either the pulpit or the rostrum.

Very English were the nine colonial colleges—and also, despite the War of Independence, the numerous colleges that were founded in the new republic. Harvard was modelled on Emmanuel College, Cambridge, and Cambridge graduates were energetically active in shaping that new college at Cambridge, Massachusetts. Queen's College, Oxford, was emulated by the College of William and Mary.

"With rare exception the American college for many years was significantly shaped by the English universities," Frederick Rudolph writes in his history of American colleges and universities.

> Yet, if the immediate ancestor of the American colonial college was the English university, the lineage was ancient. The American college was also conceived as a descendant of the schools of Hebrew prophets. . . . It was altogether impossible, however, to disguise or ignore the debt owed the English universities, for the colonial curriculum was the proper amalgam of the medieval arts and sciences and of Renaissance interest in the study of literature and belles-lettres. The fundamental discipline was Latin—the language of the law, of the church, of medicine; the language through which the translations of Aristotle from the Greek had dominated the medieval course of study; the language in which Aristotle's philosophies—natural, moral, and mental—entered the medieval universities. Taking its place beside Latin was Greek, the language of the new humanism, of Renaissance learning; it brought Homer and Hesiod, Greek lyrics and idylls, into the experience of the educated man. . .
>
> The English university was everywhere a fountain of inspiration and influence.[9]

So matters stood until the War of Independence, which of course interrupted America's higher education for some years. After that soon followed a passing enthusiasm, especially among students, for the French Revolution, with its radical slogans and Rousseauistic notions in education. But a more serious threat to the American version of British education, with its strong emphasis upon moral philosophy and its classical and Christian curriculum, was the innovating mentality of Thomas Jefferson and his followers, at once Francophile and utilitarian. This returns us to the subject of the very Anglican and very English College of William and Mary.

In 1779, while governor of Virginia, Jefferson strongly urged adoption of a bill in the Virginia legislature which would have turned William and Mary into a state institution, with the intention of converting it into the first University of Virginia, and vastly altering its program of study. The College at Williamsburg then had six professorships: Hebrew and Scripture; Theology and Apologetics; Rhetoric, Logic, and Ethics; Physics, Metaphysics, and Mathematics; Latin and Greek; and the School for Indian Boys. Jefferson would have swept away the first two of these chairs, regarding theology as superstition. The bill in the legislature failed, but in his capacity as a member of the College's board of visitors, Jefferson contrived to attain his end for the most part. Daniel Boorstin summarizes Jefferson's design:

> Jefferson had proposed changes in the professorships to make them more suitable to American conditions. The old subjects were: Greek and Latin; mathematics, moral philosophy, and divinity. The subjects which he recommended in their place were: law and police, anatomy and medicine; natural philosophy and mathematics; moral philosophy and the law of nature and of nations; fine arts; and modern languages. Jefferson urged that an endowment which originally had been given to support missionaries to the Indians should be employed instead to finance new expeditions to gather anthropological data.

He desired that there be taught only "useful and practicable studies, agriculture especially—and the Anglo-Saxon language, too, on the ground that it would teach Virginians to understand the source of their liberties. Abandoning the attempt to have the state govern William and Mary, he founded the University of Virginia."[10]

Disliking England, Jefferson aspired to Gallicize American higher education in some degree, but gained no ground in this endeavor. He recommended to President Washington that the United States acquire the Swiss School at Geneva, remove it to the United States, and convert it into a national university. Unsympathetic, Washington commented that there would occur difficulties with a staff that spoke French instead of English, that not all professors from Geneva might be gentlemen of good character, and that it would be undesirable to exclude able professors from other lands.

By 1801, Rousseau was being studied, along with Locke and Montesquieu, at William and Mary; but the Terror of 1794 in France had put an end to American idealizing of French radical theories and actions, and the British model of the higher learning was not supplanted by French designs.

The utilitarian ambitions of Jefferson and many other American democrats, nevertheless, worked to undermine the curricula of American colleges, founded on the classical languages and classical literature, as they had existed in the eighteenth century. "Usefulness" gradually subverted, especially in the new state universities, the older (and very British) aim of developing a class of gentlemen leaders, clerical and lay, through the systematic imparting of a measure of wisdom and virtue. Religious studies were deliberately excluded by Jefferson from his University of Virginia, and in general the crop of state universities looked down their noses at theology. If nowhere effaced, classical studies and religious studies declined, although enjoying some sanctuary in the independent colleges.

However battered by utilitarianism, egalitarianism, and (during the 1870s and later) Germanic theories of higher learning that conflicted with British educational traditions, the British influence upon American colleges and universities continued throughout the nineteenth century, and revived considerably in the twentieth century. To develop among the rising generation a philosophical habit of mind; to seek an ethical end through an intellectual means—such was the British tradition of the development of the mind. The British university labored to wake the reason and the moral imagination of the person for the person's own sake, through certain disciplines of the intellect. And, in the British tradition, the American colleges had expected that their graduates would address themselves unselfishly to the spiritual and social needs of their neighborhood, their state, their country.

In the better liberal arts colleges of the United States during the closing decade of the twentieth century, and in certain schools and departments of the sounder universities, some scholars still endeavor to impart a measure of wisdom and virtue, in the British concept of learning. They believe that no better way has been discovered to achieve an understanding of the human condition, or to envision a humane society. This is a British legacy, running back to Sir Thomas Elyot's *Boke named the Gouvernour* (1531) and earlier.

In school and in college, the British approach as transmitted to America had been exacting—which had not made it popular with egalitarians. The primary method of learning was the close study of certain great writings. (That plan has inspired the numerous "Great Books" programs in American colleges during the past several decades.) Consider the program at Boston Latin School (an institution that still functions, if not with so impressive a curriculum) in the year 1710:

"A boy who had reached the seventh year on this ladder of learning was reading Cicero's orations, Justinian, the Latin and Greek New Testaments, Isocrates, Homer, Hesiod, Vergil, Horace, Juvenal, and dialogues in Godwin's *Roman Antiquities*, as well as turning the Psalms into Latin verse. The last-named accomplishment was sometimes omitted by special permission."[11]

It may be objected that such a program was not useful—except as a means of understanding the greatness and the tragedy of the human condition, acquiring the art of rhetoric, coming to understand the consolations of religion, and learning about great exemplars.

Formal education in the United States still—if it is effectual—owes much to British precedent and precept. "British culture has demonstrated a remarkable vitality," the historian Louis B. Wright wrote in 1955,

and an even more remarkable capacity for the assimilation and transformation of other cultures into the British pattern. . . . Many races and nationalities contributed to the stream of settlers who went West, and many influences modified the mode of life which they adopted, but the vigor of British culture was such that it gave to all the cities and towns along the route of the westward migration a characteristic stamp. Different as are Philadelphia, New York, Boston, Cincinnati, Lexington, Indianapolis, St. Louis, and Seattle, they all have a common denominator that goes back to the seventeenth century and the stock of ideas that British settlers brought with them.[12]

Just so. The ideas and the mores of yesteryear's British people still work among Americans. Indeed the communication of the dead is tongued with fire beyond the language of the living.

Notes

1. This estimate is from *The Public Papers of George Clinton*, governor of New York. For differing estimates, see Evarts B. Greene and Virginia D. Harrington, *American Population before the Federal Census of 1790* (New York: Columbia University Press, 1932), 1–8. Statistics for 1790 are to be found in *Historical Statistics of the United States, Colonial Times to 1957*, and later editions (Washington, D.C.: United States Department of Commerce).
2. Alexis de Tocqueville, *Democracy in America*, edited by J. P. Mayer and translated by George Lawrence (Garden City, N.Y.: Doubleday Anchor Books, 1969), 287, 305–8.
3. A one-volume study of religion in the United States is Martin E. Marty's *Pilgrims in Their Own Land* (Boston: Little, Brown, 1984). For the religious persuasions

of delegates to the Constitutional Convention, see M. E. Bradford, *A Worthy Company: Brief Lives of the Framers of the United States Constitution* (Marlborough, N.H.: Plymouth Rock Foundation, 1982).

4. Tocqueville, *Democracy*, 290–93.

5. Journals, diaries, and correspondence of a good many interesting men and women who observed the United States during the formative decades are readily available. See, for instance, Isaac Weld, Jr., *Travels through the States of North America and the Provinces of Upper & Lower Canada during the Years 1795, 1796, & 1797* (published, fourth edition, 1807; reprint, 2 vols., New York: Augustus Kelley, 1970). For an Englishwoman's mordant criticisms of American mores and manners in 1828, see Mrs. Trollope's *Domestic Manners of the Americans* (1832), with an introduction by James E. Mooney (Barre, Massachusetts: Imprint Society, 1968). For the moving letters of a Virginian politician of genius, near his end when Tocqueville visited America, see *Collected Letters of John Randolph of Roanoke to Dr. John Brockenbrough, 1812-1833*, with an introduction by Kenneth Shorey (New Brunswick, N.J.: Transaction Books, 1988).

6. Henry Adams, "American Ideals," vol. I, chapter 6 of his brilliant eight-volume *History of the United States during the Administrations of Jefferson and Madison*. In Herbert Agar's abridgement of that work, *The Formative Years* (London: Collins, 1948), vol. I, 95.

7. Tocqueville, *Democracy*, 241.

8. David Hackett Fischer, *Albion's Seed: Four British Folkways in America* (New York: Oxford University Press, 1989), 6–7. Professor Fischer plans to publish several more volumes in this innovating cultural history of the United States.

9. Frederick Rudolph, *The American College and University: a History* (New York: Knopf, 1962), 24–26.

10. Daniel Boorstin, *The Lost World of Thomas Jefferson* (New York: Henry Holt, 1948), 217–18. See also Richmond Beale Davis, *Intellectual Life in Jefferson's Virginia, 1790–1830* (Knoxville: University of Tennessee Press, 1972), 46–69.

11. Richard M. Gummere, *The American Colonial Mind and the Classical Tradition* (Cambridge, Mass.: Harvard University Press, 1963), 57.

12. Louis B. Wright, *Culture on the Moving Frontier* (Bloomington: Indiana University Press, 1955), 13–14. See also Wright's *The First Gentlemen of Virginia: Intellectual Qualities of the Early Colonial Ruling Class* (Charlottesville: University Press of Virginia, 1964).

6

Renewing a Shaken Culture

The Need for Continuity

What is called *order*, a word signifying harmonious arrangement, has two aspects when we discuss the diverse cultures of humankind. The first of these is order in the soul: what is called moral order. The second of these is order of the commonwealth: what is called constitutional order. In both its aspects, order stands endangered today, requiring vigorous defense.

Six decades ago, in *The Revolt of the Masses*, Jose Ortega y Gasset wrote that American civilization could not long survive any catastrophe to European society. This remains true, and particularly true with respect to Britain. America's higher culture, and the American civil social order, are derived from institutions and concepts that arose to the east of the Atlantic Ocean. Americans are part of a great continuity and essence.

America and Britain and their cultural dependencies share a common religious heritage, a common history in large part, a common pattern of law and politics, and a common body of great literature. Yet American citizens and British subjects cannot be wholly confident that their order will endure forever. It is possible to exhaust moral and social capital; a society relying altogether upon its patrimony soon may find itself bankrupt. With civilization, as with the human body, conservation and renewal are possible only if healthful change and reinvigoration occur from age to age. It is by no means certain that our present moral and constitutional order is providing sufficiently for its own future. Modern men pay a great deal of attention to material and technological means, but little attention to the instruments by which any generation must fulfill its part in the contract of eternal society.

Twentieth-century mankind, in Britain and in America, have tended to be contemptuous of the past; yet they contribute little enough of their own, except in technology and applied sciences, toward the preservation of a tolerable order, let alone its improvement. The facile optimism of the nineteenth and early twentieth centuries is much diminished nowadays, but this does not signify that naive notions of inevitable Progress have been supplanted by serious reflection on the problem of how to conserve and to renew our cultural patrimony. The present threat to the inner order and the outer order comes as much from indifference, apathy, and selfishness as it comes from totalist political powers. Pessimism for pessimism's sake is as fatuous as is optimism for optimism's sake. Grim symptoms may be discerned of an absolute decline of the higher culture in both America and Britain, and also symptoms of a decline of the ties that have joined the English-speaking cultures on either side of the Atlantic. How may decay be arrested?

In any age, some people revolt against their own inheritance of order—and soon find themselves plunged into what Edmund Burke called "the antagonist world of madness, discord, vice, confusion, and unavailing sorrow." Near the end of the twentieth century, the number of such enemies to order has become alarming. A spirit of defiance or biting criticism that may be healthful, when confined to a creative minority, can become perilous if it is taken up unimaginatively by a popular majority. To the folk who rebel against their patrimony of moral and constitutional order, that legacy seems a burden—when in truth it is a footing. Cultural restoration, like charity, begins at home; and so I touch here upon symptoms of neglect of the common inheritance of America.

Religious faith, whether Catholic, Protestant, or Judaic, seems enfeebled in the United States. Many of the clergy tend markedly toward a sentimental and humanitarian application of religious teachings; they incline toward the radical alteration of society at the expense of the transcendent ends of religion and of any personal obedience to moral teachings.

As for the legacy of ordered liberty, there too one finds cause for misgiving. Even among judges and lawyers, one encounters a growing disregard of the old principles of justice and jurisprudence; and one encounters, too, an overwhelming tendency toward concentration of power in centralized governments.

The causes of such drifts may be found, in part, in the gradual substitution of "pragmatic" standards for old principles of jurisprudence and inherited political institutions. With few exceptions, schools of law have encouraged this progress. There may come to pass the triumph of what Eric Voegelin called "theoretical illiteracy" in law and politics. A university student of considerable native intelligence inquires of me why checks and balances are at all desirable in politics. Why should we not simply train up an elite of governmental administrators, he inquires, trust to their good will and abilities, and let them manage the concerns of the nation?

This growing naïveté, born of an ignorance of the political and legal institutions of the British-American culture, too often passes unchallenged by disciples of the pragmatic and technical methodologies dominant in schools of public administration and in governmental research. This simplicity also reflects a wondrous unawareness of human nature and of statecraft. It is the attitude that Lord Percy of Newcastle denominated "totalist democracy"—a trust in an abstraction called The People, combined with an unquestioning faith in The Expert.[1]

Theoretical illiteracy in politics and jurisprudence is paralleled by a decline of true apprehension of humane letters. In the Anglo-American culture, the study of great literature has pursued an ethical end through an intellectual means. The improvement of reason and conscience for the person's own sake, and the incidental improvement of society thereby, was the object of the traditional literary disciplines. The present generation of schoolchildren is expected, instead, to "learn to live with all the world, in one global village"—a consummation to be achieved, perhaps, by scissors-and-paste projects.

When poetry is replaced by "communication skills" and narrative history by vague sociological generalizations, the intricate patrimony of general culture is threatened. There exist professors of education who argue that no young person ought to read any book more than half a century old. The imaginative and rational disciplines, so painfully cultivated over centuries, can be permanently injured by a generation or two of neglect and contempt.

Modern men and women live in an age in which the expectation of change often seems greater than the expectation of continuity. In any order worthy of the name, men and women must be something better than the flies of a summer; generation must link with generation. Some people, in this closing decade of the twentieth century, are doing what is in their power to preserve a common heritage. This is not a work that can be accomplished through fresh positive laws or through the creation of new international commissions. Yet if a people forget the ashes of their fathers and the temples of their gods, the consequences soon will be felt in the laws and in international affairs. Cultural continuity lacking, there remains small point in political tinkering with a body social that has become exhausted spiritually and intellectually.

A French aphorism instructs us that the more things change, the more they are the same. We fight over again, generation after generation, the battle to maintain the inner order and the outer. As T. S. Eliot wrote, there are no lost causes because there are no gained causes. Say not the struggle naught availeth. In defense of the order into which we have been born, one may reaffirm the counsel of Edgar, in *King Lear*:

> Take head of the foul fiend; obey thy parents; keep thy word justly; swear not; commit not with man's sworn spouse; set not thy sweet heart on proud array. . . . Keep thy foot out of brothels, thy hand out of plackets, thy pen from lenders' books, and defy the foul fiend.

From Shakespeare, as from other most memorable dead, comes the energy that sustains people in a time of tribulations. The order, inner and outer, of our common culture is defended not by the living merely, but by the valiant dead as well.

Challenge and Response

From time to time, during this twentieth century, some American voices have been raised in dispraise of America's inheritance of British culture. One such assault occurred about the middle forties; it was renewed a decade later. Even some American scholars of good repute suggest that it would be well to drop from formal instruction most of our baggage of British literature, and to concentrate instead upon native American verse and prose; certain language associations embrace this line: buy the home-grown product! In effect these literary nationalists advocate a cultural Tariff of Abominations.

Dr. Louis B. Wright, then director of the Folger Shakespeare Library in Washington, took up his cudgel about 1952 in defense of a civilized heritage, against academic allies of barbarism. In his lively book *Culture on the Moving Frontier* (written while he was visiting Patten Professor at Indiana University, a post later enjoyed by this present writer) Dr. Wright repeatedly and persuasively digressed from his narrative to point out the essentially British character of American institutions and the American realm of reason and of art:

> Modern America is so polyglot, and social historians have devoted so much attention in recent years to analyzing and describing the multifarious European, Asiatic, and African influences in the development of American life, that we are now in danger of underestimating and even forgetting the oldest, the most persistent, and the most vigorous strain in our cultural inheritance. Great Britain's influence is still so strong that it subtly determines qualities of mind and character in Americans who cannot claim a drop of Anglo-Saxon blood. . . . If there were no other legacy from the past except the English language and its literature, that alone would be sufficient to explain the durability and strength of the tradition.[2]

Four decades after Professor Wright reproved thus the Goths and Vandals within the Ivory Tower, a new horde of adversaries is bent upon deconstructing the edifice of Anglo-American culture. The principal accrediting associations of the United States, indeed, have menaced colleges and universities with disaccreditation unless they promptly proceed to enter upon programs of multiculturalism, permeating the whole curriculum; and various academic presidents and deans have supinely submitted to this intellectual bullying; but the federal Secretary of Education has rebuffed these barbarous educationists somewhat, threatening *them* in turn with governmental disaccreditation of unjust accreditors.

One encounters in today's American education, truly, a great deal of dullness at every level, and much intellectual provinciality, too. Ever since the Second World War, indeed, oddly enough, American schooling, from kindergarten through graduate school, has sunk farther and farther into the provinciality of place and time, so that the rising generation grows up unicultural, notably ignorant of other countries and other cultures, despite the tremendous ascendancy of the United States in world affairs.

Six decades ago, when this present writer was enrolled in a public grade school not far from great railway yards outside Detroit, nobody thought of demanding multiculturalism: we already possessed that in our school. In geography class, we learned a great deal about the cultures of five continents; we were very interested. Many of us, a few years later, enrolled (during high school) in three years of history: ancient, modern, and American. At least half of us took two years of language, either Latin or French, with corresponding instruction about Roman civilization or French culture; some pupils finished four years of foreign language. Our intelligent courses in English and American literature helped to redeem us from what T. S. Eliot called "the provincialism of time." We were much aware of diversity in the world and in our own country.

Today the radical multiculturalists complain, or rather shout, that African, Asian, and Latin American cultures have been shamefully neglected in North America's schools. In that they are correct enough. In many primary, intermediate, and high schools nowadays—aye, in colleges, too—the offering in the discipline of history amounts only to a whirlwind "Survey of World History" (with Good Guys and Bad Guys occasionally pointed out by the teacher, amidst the violent dust storm), and perhaps a year of American history, often ideologically distorted. As for geography, that virtually has gone by the board; at least one famous state university, a few years ago, swept away altogether its department of geography. Even at boarding schools of good repute and high fees, the teaching of humane letters is very nearly confined to reading and discussing some recent ephemeral novels.

Sixty years ago, most school pupils were taught a good deal about the people and the past of Bolivia, Morocco, China, India, Egypt, Guatemala, and other lands. They even learnt about Eskimo and Aleut cultures. Nowadays pupils are instructed in the disciplines of home economics, driver education, sex education, and the sterile abstractions of Social Stu. Formerly all pupils studied for several years the principal British and American poets, essayists, novelists, and dramatists—this with the purpose of developing their moral imagination. Nowadays they are assigned the prose of "relevance" and "current awareness" at most schools. Indeed a great deal of alleged "education," either side of the Ocean Sea, requires medication or surgery.

But what the curious sect of multiculturalists prescribe, in Britain as in America, is poison. There is reason to suspect that such multiculturalists as Leonard Jeffries, a black radical professor at the City College of New York, hope to bring down the whole edifice of pedagogy—so as to hold among the ruins perpetual "rap sessions" about indignities once suffered by blacks.*

Yet suppose that the multiculturalists were sincere in their professions of desire to redress the balance by reducing emphases upon "Eurocentric" and British culture, and introducing new programs to describe other cultures that have affected the United States—why, how might the thing be accomplished? The number of hours in an academic day is limited. How would a multicultural curriculum deal with the worthy contributions of Armenians, Syrians, Lebanese, Iraqui Chaldeans, Russians, Ukrainians, Poles, Serbs, Maltese, Croats, Puerto Ricans, Czechs, Chinese, Vietnamese, Mexicans, Hungarians, and a score of other "minorities" that inhabit the city of Detroit, say? Early in 1991, the Detroit School Board instructed publishers of textbooks that the Board would give short shrift to any school manuals not fully emphasizing the contributions of Afro-Americans to American culture. Are textbooks for instruction, or are they to become merely devices for "increasing the self-esteem" of ethnic groups?

Even before multiculturalism was taken seriously by anybody, it was sufficiently difficult to publish a textbook that objectively dealt with its subject. The present writer, a decade ago, was editing a series of social science manuals. In a history textbook, it had been found prudent to insert a chapter on the Mongols—giving those devastators equal space and classroom time with Hellenes and Romans. In that chapter appeared the phrase "the charge of the barbarian horsemen." Our textbooks were printed and distributed by a commercial textbook publisher, acting for our council. A woman editor of that firm instructed me, "There may have been women among them. Change your phrase to 'the charge of the barbarian horsepersons.'" I replied to her that in historical fact, the ferocious cavalry of Genghis Khan included no females; and that I knew of no American woman who would be gratified by being labelled a "barbarian horseperson." Such are the

---

*Jeffries it was who drafted the report "A Curriculum of Inclusion" to submit to the New York Board of Regents. During the summer of 1991, Mr. Jeffries indulged himself in denunciation of the Jews, some of them having been obstacles in his deconstructive path; his epithets opened the eyes of persons who had fancied that multiculturalism was merely an endeavor to inform the rising generation about the contributions made to American civilization by folk from many lands. Early in 1992, Jeffries was removed from his administrative post.

difficulties that arise when objective scholarship is subject to the whims of all "minorities" —and, moreover, when those "minorities" are engaged in endless warfare, one against another.

It is well to learn much about distant cultures. When a sophomore in college, this present writer spent a whole year reading rare works about travels in Africa, borrowed from the shelves of the Library of the State of Michigan—considerably to the neglect of the conventional disciplines for which he was being graded at his college. But to neglect or to repudiate the central and pervasive British culture in America would be to let the whole academic and social enterprise fall apart: "the center cannot hold; Mere anarchy is loosed upon the world. . . ."

May the Anglo-American culture, so battered by the pace of change during the twentieth century, so damaged by ideological assaults these past several decades, be restored to health? (It is one culture, really, that complex of literature and law and government and mores which still makes civilization possible in both the United States and Britain. Of the three major poets in the English language during the twentieth century—T. S. Eliot, Robert Frost, William Butler Yeats—two were American-born, a fact suggesting that British and American cultures have coalesced.) No culture endures forever: of those that have vanished, some have fallen to alien conquerors, as did Roman Britain; but most have expired in consequence of internal decay; when the cult failed, the culture presently crumbled to powder. Will the American culture and the British expire jointly "not with a bang, but a whimper?" One thinks of the Chorus of Sir Osbert Sitwell's long poem *Demos the Emperor*:

> We are the modern masters of the world,
> The arbiters, the heirs
> Of Egypt, Greece and Italy
>   (We have no time for art
>   But we know what we like!)
> We are the fulfilment of Man's promise
> The Cup-tie Final and the paper cap;
> We are the Soul of the Cash Register,
> The Secret of the Hire-Purchase System,
> The Vacuum, and the Vacuum-Cleaner.*

---

*Published in 1949.

Perhaps; and yet, as the present writer once remarked to President Nixon, great cultures commonly pass through alternating periods of decay and renewal, flickering out finally after many centuries. Byzantine civilization is our clearest instance of this process. The culture from which Anglo-American culture developed extends back more than three thousand years, to Moses and Aaron. Cultures cannot be deliberately created; they arise, rather, from the theophanic events that bring cults into existence. It remains conceivable, nevertheless, that cultures may be *reinvigorated*.

If America's British culture is to be reinvigorated, its roots must be watered. The twentieth-century guardians of that culture must reject such silliness as the multiculturalist ideology, which does nothing more than gratify little ethnic vanities. Those guardians—who are the whole class of tolerably educated Americans—must resist those ideologues of multiculturalism who would pull down the whole elaborate existing culture of this country in order to make everybody culturally equal— that is, equal in ignorance. On this point, Louis B. Wright deserves to be quoted a final time:

> For better or worse, we have inherited the fundamental qualities in our culture from the British. For that reason we need to take a long perspective of our history, a perspective which views America from at least the period of the first Tudor monarch and lets us see the gradual development of our common civilization, its transmission across the Atlantic, and its expansion and modification as it was adapted to conditions in the Western Hemisphere. We should not overlook other influences which have affected American life, influences from France, Holland, Spain, Germany, Scandinavia, and the rest of Europe, and also influences from Asia and Africa. But we must always remember that such was the vigor of British culture that it assimilated all others. That is not to say that we have been transmogrified into Englishmen, or that we are even Anglophile in sentiment. But we cannot escape an inheritance which has given us some of our sturdiest and most lasting qualities.[3]

Arnold Toynbee instructs us that cultures develop, and civilizations arise, by the process of challenge and response. Some threat to a culture's survival may occur; if the culture vigorously surmounts that challenge, the culture will grow in strength; but if the challenge is so formidable as to damage or distort the culture—why, the threatened culture becomes stunted and possibly succumbs altogether.

The ideology called multiculturalism might benefit American society, after all—in the sense that it is a challenge (if a foolish challenge) to the friends of America's inherited culture. If the response to the multiculturalist threat is healthy, it should rouse again among Americans an apprehension of the high merits of the literature, the language, the laws, the political institutions, and the mores that Americans have received, in the course of four centuries, from the British people. For if a civilization never is challenged, that civilization tends to sink into apathy—and slowly to dissolution.

Multiculturalism is animated by envy and hatred. Some innocent persons have assumed that a multicultural program in schools would consist of discussing the latest number of *National Geographic* in a classroom. That is not at all what the multiculturalists intend. Detesting the achievements of Anglo-American culture, they propose to substitute for real history and real literature—and even for real natural science—an invented myth that all things good came out of Africa and Asia (chiefly Africa).[4]

Intellectually, multiculturalism is puny—and anticultural. Such power as the multiculturalist ideologues possess is derived from political manipulation: that is, claiming to speak for America's militant "minorities." These ideologues take advantage of the sentimentality of American liberals, eager to placate such "minorities" by granting them whatever they demand. But what fanatic ideologues demand commonly is bad for the class of persons they claim to represent, as it is bad, too, for everybody else. To deny "minorities" the benefits of America's established culture would work their ruin.

"Culture, with us, ends in headache," Ralph Waldo Emerson wrote of Americans in 1841. Should the multiculturalists have their way, culture, with us Americans a century and a half later, would end in heartache—and in anarchy. But to this challenge of multiculturalism, presumably the established American culture, with its British roots, still can respond with vigor—a life-renewing response. Love of an inherited culture has the power to cast out the envy and hatred of that culture's adversaries.

Notes

1. See Lord Percy of Newcastle, *The Heresy of Democracy* (Chicago: Henry Regnery, 1955), particularly chap. 1, "The Birth of Democracy."
2. Louis B. Wright, *Culture on the Moving Frontier* (Bloomington: Indiana University Press, 1955), 15.

3. Wright, *Culture*, 241.
4. For the fraudulent character of multiculturalist "scholarship," see, for instance, Gleaves Whitney, "Is the American Academy Racist?" (a criticism of Martin Bernal's *Black Athena: The Afroasiatic Roots of Classical Civilization*) in *The University Bookman* 30, no. 2 (1990): 4–15.

Appendix:

What Did Americans Inherit from the Ancients?

It was British scholars and schoolmasters who imparted to the Americans of the thirteen colonies a knowledge of classical languages and literature, Greek and Roman history and politics and law. A translation of Plutarch's *Lives of the Noble Greeks and Romans* often stood on an American's bookshelf alongside the Bible; and the character of leading Americans was formed by both books. The influence of Greek and Roman literature upon the people of British North America is well described in Richard M. Gummere's book *The American Colonial Mind and the Classical Tradition.*[1] Second only to great English literature's influence upon yesteryear's Americans, classical philosophy and drama and rhetoric helped to shape American thought and mores.

Although those Americans who attended British universities, or the few American colleges established during the colonial era, acquired a good mastery of Ciceronian Latin often, and a tolerable acquaintance with ancient Greek, in general Americans read Plato and Aristotle, Plutarch and Livy, Sophocles and Seneca, in the great English translations published during the Tudor reigns, as the English commenced settling North America. Thus an English flavor permeated even the literary legacy Americans received from the ancient world.[2]

Just what is this classical patrimony that much influenced both the thought and the action of the people of the thirteen colonies, and that was cherished in the United States well into the twentieth century? To Europeans living west of the Elbe or south of the Danube, the remains of classical civilization are visible even today: intelligent observers are aware of a continuity extending over many generations. Englishmen can look upon Roman masonry at York, Chester, Colchester, and even today's London. For that matter, Roman ruins survive from the Atlantic shore of the Iberian peninsula all the way to the Euphrates, or from Scotland to Morocco. People who speak Romance tongues cannot be altogether unaware of the Roman past, nor can Greeks forget their distant cultural ancestors. But in North America, neither monuments of antiquity nor the roots of language can evoke memories of civilizations broken, yet somehow working through Americans in ghostly fashion. Nevertheless, Americans pay public homage to long-dead Greeks and Romans. Why is the public architecture of the District of Columbia still dominated by classical columns and domes? Why do Americans still pay some lip service to the disciplines of the humanities, the sources of which may be traced back to Greece six centuries before Christ?

It should be confessed that in some respects our debt to the ancients is not quite so great as certain historians and professors of politics would have us believe. The "lamp of experience" that Patrick Henry held high was not, in any positive and immediate fashion about 1775, the political experience of the Greeks and the Romans. That political and social experience "by which my feet are guided" (in Henry's famous phrase) was the British experience and the experience of British subjects in the colonies. Then as now, the great mass of men and women were guided by received custom and convention, not by Hebraic or Greek or Latin texts. Only the well-schooled, in any literate culture, are much influenced in their conduct by learned writings of yesteryear. Although Patrick Henry read much, he was not ·moved mightily by intellectual abstractions.[3]

In the Bicentennial years, a good deal was said about the Greek roots of American democracy, the model of the Roman Republic for Americans, and that sort of thing. (Too little was said about the Hebraic and Hellenic patrimony of moral order.)

In truth America's political *institutions* owe next to nothing to the ancient world—although American modes of *thinking* about politics indeed were influenced, two centuries ago, by Greek and Roman philosophers long dead.

One learns much about constitutions from reading Plato and Aristotle and Polybius; constitutions monarchic, aristocratic, democratic;

about oligarchies and timocracies; about tyrannies and kingships; about the polity, that blending of types of government. The educated Americans of the generation to which the Framers of the Constitution belonged studied the books of the Greeks and the Romans. But those books could not teach the Americans very much about constitutions that might be applied practically to the infant Republic of the United States.

For the people of the thirteen colonies had known almost from the first English settlements the institutions of representative government; while the ancient world had known nothing of that sort. Representative government, indeed, was what the War of Independence had been about. Only through some system of representation could a far-spreading United States of America be conceivable. Even the most redoubtable Anti-Federalist did not fancy that the American Republic could consist of a league of infant city-states; a Congress there must be, and that Congress must be a *representative* assembly.

For Greek politics in ancient times were the politics of city-states for the most part, compact in territory, limited in population; and in the Greek democracies the entire body of male citizens was able to assemble in a forum for making public decisions of the gravest sort—sometimes foolish decisions with ghastly consequences. The United States, on the contrary, was a vast expanse of territory in which the few cities, in 1787, counted for little. And the Americans, unlike the Greeks, had the printing press to inform their democratic society. Many other differences existed.

Anyone who studies history seriously is liable to be disheartened by the repeated disastrous failures of human attempts to achieve a tolerable measure of order and justice and freedom, for any great length of time. Sir Ernest Barker, an eminent English professor of politics, commented on the views of that great historian of law Sir Henry Maine: "History has with Maine, what it tends to have with many of us, a way of numbing generous emotions. All things have happened already; nothing much came of them before; nothing much can be expected of them now."[4]

Maine, writing in the last quarter of the nineteenth century, knew from his studies in ancient law how the democratic republics of classical Greece had failed. A hundred years before Maine wrote, the authors of the *Federalist Papers*, and the other Framers of the American Constitution, had perceived that Americans could not find in the history of the Greek city-states any satisfactory model of a good constitution.

Study of Greek and Latin literature, and of the ancient world's history and politics, loomed much larger in American education during the latter half of the eighteenth century than it does in American education today. Most of the Framers at one time or another, in translation or in the original Greek or Latin, had read such ancient authors as Herodotus, Thucydides, Plato, Aristotle, Polybius, Cicero, Livy, and Plutarch—philosophers and historians who described the constitutions of the Greek and Roman civilizations. But from such study the American leaders of the War of Independence and the constitution-making era learned, by their own account, chiefly what political blunders of ancient times ought to be avoided by the Republic of the United States.

For the Greek city-states of the sixth and fifth and fourth centuries before Christ never succeeded in developing enduring constitutions that would give them order and justice and freedom. Civil war within those city-states was the rule, rather than the exception, class against class, family against family, faction against faction. And when half of those cities went to war against the other half, in the ruinous Peloponnesian struggle, during the last three decades of the fifth century—why, Greek civilization never wholly recovered from that disaster.

Leading Americans did study closely the old Greek constitutions. In his *Defence of the Constitutions of Government of the United States of America* (published in 1787, on the eve of America's Great Convention), John Adams examines critically twelve ancient democratic republics, three ancient aristocratic republics, and three ancient monarchial republics—and finds them all inferior to the political system of the new Republic of the United States. Alexander Hamilton, James Madison, and John Jay, the authors of the *Federalist Papers*, often referred to "the turbulent democracies of ancient Greece" (Madison's phrase) and to other ancient constitutions. In general, those three American statesmen found the political systems of Greece and Rome "as unfit for the imitation, as they are repugnant to the genius of America" (again, Madison's phrase). Old James Monroe, long after he had been president of the United States, wrote his little book *The People, the*

Sovereigns, finding the ancient constitutions of Athens, Sparta, and Carthage woefully defective when contrasted with the Constitution of the United States, in which the sovereign people conferred power upon governors.[5] The American Framers and the early statesmen of the Republic, whether Federalists or Republicans, were no admirers of classical political structures.

Eighteenth-century Americans did respect Solon, the lawgiver of Athens in the sixth century before Christ. But Solon's good constitution for his native city had lasted merely some thirty years before a tyrant seized power in Athens. Nor did ancient political theory, as distinct from institutions, often obtain American approbation: John Adams wrote that he had learned from reading Plato two things only: "First, that Franklin's ideas of exempting husbandmen and mariners, &c., from the depredations of war, were borrowed from him; and second, that sneezing is a cure for the hiccough."[6]

Ancient Greek culture indeed did help to shape education in America, but Greek constitutions had next to no part in shaping the Constitution of the United States, nor the constitutions of the several states—except so far as Greek constitutional flaws suggested what Framers at Philadelphia and elsewhere ought *not* to adopt.

The Roman Republic was taken somewhat more seriously by leading Americans in the 1780s. The English word *constitution* is derived from the Latin *constitutio*, signifying a collection of laws or ordinances made by a Roman emperor. American boys at any decent school in the eighteenth century studied the orations and the life of Marcus Tullius Cicero, the defender of the Roman Republic in its declining years. The Roman term "Senate" was applied by the American Framers to the more select house of the legislative branch of their federal government—although the method for selecting senators in America would be very different from what it had been in Rome.

For the American constitutional delegates at Philadelphia, the most interesting feature of the Roman Republican constitution was its system of checks upon the power of men in high public authority, and its balancing of power among different public offices. The Americans had learned of these devices from the *History* by Polybius, a Greek statesman who had lived long in Rome—under compulsion. The two Roman consuls, or executives; the Roman Senate, made up of rich and powerful men who had served in several important offices before being made senators; the Roman assembly, or gathering of the common people—these three bodies exercised separate powers. And the Roman constitution (an "unwritten" one) included other provisions for preventing any one class from putting down other classes, and for preserving the republican form of government. Praised by Polybius as the best constitution of his age, this Roman constitutional system was bound up with a beneficial body of civil law, and with "the high old Roman virtue"— the traditional Roman morality, with its demand for the performance of duties and for determined courage.

The actual forms of checks and balances that the Americans incorporated into their Constitution in 1787 were derived from English precedent and from American colonial experience, rather than directly from the Roman model. Instances from the history of the Roman Republic, nevertheless, often were cited by the Framers and by other leading Americans of that time as reinforcement for the American concept and reality of political checks and balances. And the Americans' vision of a great and growing republic owed much to the annals of the Roman Republic.

In consequence of the long civil wars of Roman factions in the first century before Christ, the Republic fell, to be supplanted by the Roman empire. This Roman experience, and the decadence that oppressed Roman civilization as the centuries elapsed, were much in the minds of American leaders near the end of the eighteenth century. The grim consequences of political centralization under the Empire did something to discourage the notion of an American government that would be central rather than federal—much as the Greeks' disunity was remarked by some delegates as a warning against leaving the American Republic a mere confederation. Besides, Roman struggles of class against class reminded Americans that they must seek to reconcile different classes through their own constitutional structure.

Thus Rome's political and moral example was a cautionary lesson to Americans of the early Republic. Gibbon's grand history *The Decline and Fall of the Roman Empire* had been published between 1776 and 1783, the period of the American Revolution, and its details were vivid in the minds of the delegates at Philadelphia.

Yet it will not do to make too much of the influence of the Roman constitution upon the Constitution of the United States, two thousand years after Polybius wrote in praise of Roman character and institutions. The more immediate and practical examples of constitutional success were the British and the colonial American political structures; and the American Republic was joined with Britain and with her own colonial past by a continuity of culture that much exceeded the Americans' link with old Rome, so distant and so remote in time.

In ancient times and in modern, the central problem of political constitutions has been this: how to reconcile the claims of authority with the claims of freedom. In any tolerable society, there must exist a permanent authority that maintains order and enforces the laws. Also, in any tolerable society, individuals and voluntary groups ought to enjoy considerable freedom. If authority (whether a government or some other general authority) claims too much, despotism may come to pass. If too much is claimed for personal freedom, anarchy may result. The states of the ancient world never wholly succeeded, in their constitutions, in satisfactorily balancing authority and liberty.

It was the aspiration of the delegates at Philadelphia, in 1787, to reconcile the need for a strong federal government with the demand for much personal liberty and for guarantees of state and local powers. They could not find in the history of the ancient world any model that might achieve this purpose. In 1866, nine decades after the Great Convention at Philadelphia, Orestes Brownson—one of the more interesting of America's political thinkers—would write in his book *The American Republic* that America's mission under God was to realize the true idea of the political state or nation; to give flesh to that concept of the commonwealth

> which secures at once the authority of the public and the freedom of the individual— the sovereignty of the people without social despotism, and individual freedom without anarchy. . . . The Greek and Roman republics asserted the state to the detriment of individual freedom; modern republics either do the same, or assert individual freedom to the detriment of the state. The American Republic has been instituted by Providence to realize the freedom of each with advantage to the other.[7]

Certainly such a high ambition, surpassing the political achievements of the ancient world, was the spirit of 1787 at Philadelphia.

If, then, the Greeks and the Romans bequeathed to America no political institutions—why, what is America's inheritance from the ancient world? Primarily, that patrimony is a body of great literature. The poets, the philosophers, the rhetoricians, the historians, the biographers, the satirists, the dramatists of the ancient world move us still; their aphorisms are embedded in our schooling, their descriptions of the human condition tell us what is tragic and what pathetic. Aye, the theologians of the late centuries of the Graeco-Roman culture move us, too; for Augustine of Hippo and Gregory the Great were men of the classical culture, and so were other Fathers of the Church, West and East.

Does not the preceding paragraph omit the patrimony of justice and law that has come down to our time for Greece, and more especially from Roman, sources? No, I am not ignoring that great inheritance; I am merely pointing out that this is a literary, rather than an institutional, legacy, especially when one refers to the laws of the United States and of other countries basically English in their legal institutions. British and American jurisprudence was much influenced, formerly at least, by the writings of Plato, Aristotle, and Cicero; and British judges, reading Roman law surreptitiously despite repeated fulminations from the Crown, were not immune from the doctrines of Gaius, Ulpian, and the Corpus Juris. But obviously the juridical system of the United States is not copied directly from the Roman system of courts and procedures, any more that the Constitution of the United States is an embodiment of Greek political philosophy.

So it is through books of one sort or another that the ancient world moves us moderns. Once upon a time, well-educated men and women could read those books in the original Latin or Greek; but in the present century, and more particularly during the past seven decades, the proportion of people well acquainted with the classical languages has declined fearfully. In translation, however, the books of the greater writers of ancient times continue to work upon minds and consciences, if not so strongly as such writers did two centuries ago, when the Americans accepted "a more perfect Union."

Why is it that educational authorities, down to this writer's own youthful years, believed the teaching of the great literature of Greece and Rome highly important for the enlargement of wisdom and virtue, mind and character? Why was it that the British pattern of schooling, developed during the sixteenth and seventeenth and eighteenth centuries and continued little altered at the better schools down to recent decades, consisted in large part of careful study of Plato and Aristotle, the Greek dramatists and historians, Cicero, Vergil, Horace, Livy,

Tacitus, Seneca, Plutarch? Why was it that well into the nineteenth century, even in wild Connaught, hedge schoolmasters like Yeats' Red Hanrahan went about with an inkpot hanging on a chain round the neck, a heavy copy of Vergil in a coat pocket, teaching Latin poetry to little barefoot Papist boys? Were the educational authorities of yesteryear absurdly mistaken about the importance of the ancient writers? Have today's educational authorities mercifully rescued the rising generation from servitude to the dead hand of the past, that the young may rejoice in the blessings of the new discipline of computer science?

On the contrary, the classical disciplines in schooling were immensely important, and for centuries successful. Their purpose was to bring about order in the soul and order in the commonwealth.

First, the poets and the philosophers of antiquity examined keenly the human condition. What are we mortals, and what are we to do in the short span of man's existence? Such ultimate questions were taken up boldly by both Greek and Roman writers of genius. People of the modern age were able to profit much from these discourses and disputations of some two thousand years ago, because the very remoteness in time of the ancient poets and philosophers emancipated modern readers from the tyranny of present-day passions and complexities. The Greeks and the Romans did not possess the Hebrews' treasures of the Book and the Law; but they possessed insights into human nature and even into physical nature—the theory of atoms, for instance—that people near the end of the twentieth century account for. Once this writer said to the Earl of Crawford, a considerable classical scholar, that the ancient Greeks knew everything important. "Yes," he replied, "and the question is, '*How* did they know it?'" Knowledge of ancient insight and speculation is the way to acquire a philosophical habit of mind.

Second, the literature of the ancient world was employed to form good character among the rising generation. Plutarch's heroes were exemplars for the men who framed the Constitution of the United States. In my own case, the *Meditations* of Marcus Aurelius have influenced me more strongly than has any other treatise, of any age, in any language. The high old Roman virtues were inculcated among the literate of many lands, century upon century: one might write an essay, I suppose, upon how the audacious character of the Polish nobility, say, down to very recent years, was formed in Roman molds, Latin being the language of the educated in Poland until well into the eighteenth century. Or one might trace the strong influence of Roman models upon the Spaniards—Iberia having been more Roman than Italy, in imperial times—and through the Spaniards, upon the upper classes of Latin America. Cicero's *Offices* became in medieval times a manual for the duties of the leaders of men; and although presumably no candidate for the presidency of these United States, in recent years, kept on his bedside table the *Offices*, nevertheless in subtle ways that book and the manuals of the Stoics still linger as exhortations to, or restraints upon, public men in this land—linger in ghostly fashion, transmuted through later writers or embedded in political customs. One may add that the very recent concern for restoring in American public schooling some measures to form good character has revived in certain quarters an interest in classical moral philosophy, as distinguished from religious instruction.

Third, the classical literature of jurisprudence and law obviously is a very importance part of our patrimony from Greece and Rome. The theory of justice which prevailed in the West generally until the Russian Revolution, and which still prevails after a fashion in Western Europe and the Americas, has its roots in Aristotle's doctrine of "to each his own," and in Aristotle's observation that it is unjust to treat unequal things equally. The Ciceronian teaching of natural law, though much assailed and battered since the closing years of the eighteenth century, still has vitality—if sometimes in curiously distorted forms. And of course Justinian's *Corpus Juris* reconquered Europe, gradually, for *Romanitas*—long after Rome had fallen, and spreading its power even after the fall of Constantinople. And incorporated into canon law, Roman legal principles still function within the framework of the Catholic Church and are studied in this metamorphosed form today, in the law schools of Central and Southern Europe most notable.

One might go on to describe other great ways in which the civilization dominant in the Mediterranean world, more than two millenia gone, still works among us. But time runs on, runs on. I have emphasized strongly our classical literary patrimony, and have denied that we enjoy much inheritance from Greece and Rome in our political institutions. But I do not mean to argue that no Roman influence survives in social—as distinguished from political—institutions, even to this day.

In Italy, and to some degree in Spain, it still is possible to find functioning, especially in old-fashioned towns and villages, remnants of social usages that apparently have survived many centuries of devastation and radical social alteration—even of vast demographic changes. But when I refer to social institutions, I mean something larger and more widespread that remnants of ancient folkways.

Nay, I mean, rather, to give an eminent example, the institution of the family, still most close-knit in the south of Europe, but transplanted to northern Europe also, and across the Atlantic. The Roman state never forgot that the family was the footing of all civil social order; the state was solicitous for the family's well-being—if, at the end, unsuccessful in its protections. This function of safeguarding and upholding the family passed from the dying Roman state to the emerging universal church, gradually, but most notably during the reign of Gregory the Great. Thus the Church, in medieval times and in modern, labored skillfully to nurture family loves and family duties: the institutions of classical Rome transmuted into the institutions of Christian Rome. "Rome is the power that withholds," John Henry Newman wrote—the power, in ancient times and even in our own day, which restrains men and women from the indulgence of those appetites which, given their head, would shatter the human race. The strong family has been such an institution of restraint, life-giving restraint. No-fault divorce nowadays is only one of the socially destructive assaults upon the traditional family that, in the name of emancipation, would make us all into orphans. When that restraining power of Rome is broken, Newman declared, there will come the Anti-Christ. But such prophecies are not Delphic or Cumaean.[8]

However that may be, the institution of the family comes to us in part through Rome; yet through Roman principles absorbed into Britain, and reinforced by British social experience. This filtering is true of nearly all of America's classical patrimony: Americans know it through British eyes.

Fulbert of Chartres, in medieval times, declared that we moderns— that is, the people of his own age—are dwarfs standing upon the shoulders of giants: we see farther than do the giants, but merely because we are mounted upon their shoulders. Those giants are the wise men of classical and early Christian epochs. From them Americans have inherited the order of the soul and the order of the commonwealth. If we think to liberate ourselves from the past by leaping off those giants' shoulders—why, we tumble into the ditch of unreason. If we ignore the subtle wisdom of the classical past and the British past, we are left with a thin evanescent culture, a mere film upon the surface of the deep well of the past. Those who refuse to drink of that well may be drowned in it.

Notes

1. Richard M. Gummere, *The American Colonial Mind and the Classical Tradition: Essays in Comparative Culture* (Cambridge, Massachusetts: Harvard University Press, 1963); *Seven Wise Men of Colonial America* (Cambridge, Mass.: Harvard University Press, 1967); *Seneca the Philosopher and His Modern Message* (New York: Cooper Square Publishers, 1963).
2. For such Tudor translations, see T. S. Eliot, "Seneca in Elizabethan Translation" and "Shakespeare and the Stoicism of Seneca" in Eliot, *Selected Essays, 1917-1932* (New York: Harcourt, Brace, 1932).
3. See M. E. Bradford, "According to Their Genius: Politics and the Example of Patrick Henry," in *A Better Guide than Reason: Studies in the American Revolution* (La Salle, Ill.: Sherwood Sugden, 1979).
4. Ernest Barker, *Political Thought in England from Spencer to the Present Day* (London: Williams and Norgate, 1938), 167.
5. James Monroe, *The People, the Sovereigns*, with foreword by Russell Kirk (Cumberland, Va.: James River Press, 1987).
6. John Adams, letter to Thomas Jefferson, 16 July 1814, in Charles Francis Adams (ed.), *The Life and Works of John Adams* (Boston: Little, Brown, 1856), vol. X, 102–3.
7. Orestes Brownson, *The American Republic* (facsimile edition, Clifton, N.J.: J. M. Kelly, 1872), 2–3.
8. John Henry Newman, "The Patristical Idea of Antichrist," in *Discussions and Arguments on Various Subjects* (new edition, London: Longmans, Green, 1891).

Chronology
Until the Beginning of the
Twentieth Century

446?	Angles and Saxons migrate to Britain.
563	St. Columba begins to convert the Picts of Scotland.
597	St. Augustine of Canterbury begins to convert England to Christianity.
615	Decisive Anglo-Saxon victory over Celtic British.
657?	Caedmon writes his *Hymn*, biblical paraphrases.
663	Synod of Whitby, by which Roman Christianity triumphs in Britain.
731	Bede's *Ecclesiastical History*.
787	First landing of the Vikings in England.
871	Alfred the Great becomes king of Wessex.
878	Alfred begins *The Anglo-Saxon Chronicle*.
1016	Cnut of Denmark crowned king of England.
1066	William of Normandy conquers England.
1093	St. Anselm consecrated archbishop of Canterbury.
1100	Henry I crowned king of England.
1140	*Decretum Graniani* circulated.
1170	Archbishop Thomas Becket murdered.
1215	King John of England seals Magna Carta.
1242	Knights of the shire summoned to the English Parliament.
1249	University College, Oxford, founded.
1265	Representatives of the towns summoned to the English Parliament.
1284	Peterhouse College, Cambridge, founded.
1295	"Model Parliament" summoned by Edward I of England.
1297	Confirmation of the Charters by Edward I.
1321	Death of Dante Alighieri.
1322	By the Statute of York, the Commons are recognized as an essential part of the English Parliament.
1337	The Hundred Years' War begins.

1340	By statute, taxation without consent of the English Parliament is forbidden.
1377	John Wycliffe's teaching is condemned by Pope Gregory XI.
1381	Peasants' Revolt in England.
1399	Coronation of Henry of Bolingbroke in England, with assertion of parliamentary authority over succession to the throne.
1400	Death of Geoffrey Chaucer.
1413	Papal bull issued to confirm the charter of the University of St. Andrews, Scotland.
1454	Beginning of the Wars of the Roses in England.
1480	William Caxton, first English printer, publishes *The Description of Britain*.
1485	Henry Tudor wins the English throne.
1492	Columbus reaches the West Indies.
1497	John Cabot, under patent from Henry VII, discovers the coast of North America.
1531	Sir Thomas Elyot publishes *The Boke Named the Gouvernour*.
1534	The Act of Supremacy overthrows the Catholic establishment in England.
1535	Sir Thomas More executed by Henry VIII.
1538	Henry VIII excommunicated.
1539	Cranmer's Bible published in England.
1547	King Henry VIII dies, and is succeeded by his young son Edward VI, backed by the Protestant interest.
1549	The English Book of Common Prayer is published.
1553	Edward VI dies, and is succeeded by Mary Tudor, a Catholic.
1558	Elizabeth I crowned queen of England.
1559	John Knox leads a violent reformation in Scotland, resisted by the regent, Mary of Guise, mother of Mary Queen of Scots.
1560	Catholicism is suppressed in Scotland, and the Reformed Kirk of Scotland is established.
1563	The Anglican Convocation ratifies the Thirty-Nine Articles, fixing the doctrine of the Church of England.
1582	The University of Edinburgh is founded.
1583	Sir Walter Ralegh lands in Virginia.
1587	Queen Mary Stuart is beheaded in England.
1588	Christopher Marlowe's *The tragical history of Dr. Faustus* is published.
1590	Publication of Edmund Spenser's *The Faerie Queen*.

1591	Publication of Sir Philip Sidney's *Astrophel and Stella*.
1593-1594	Part I of Richard Hooker's *Laws of Ecclesiastical Polity* is published.
1595	Ralegh makes his first expedition to the Orinoco.
1598	Publication of Ben Jonson's *Every Man in his Humour*.
1600	The East India Company is founded.
1603	James VI of Scotland, Mary Stuart's son, is crowned James I of England.
	Sir Walter Ralegh begins writing his *History of the World* while imprisoned in the Tower of London.
1607	Jamestown, in Virginia, is founded by the Virginia Company.
1608	First printing of William Shakespeare's *King Lear*.
1609	Hudson discovers the Hudson and Delaware rivers.
1611	Publication of the Authorized Version of the Bible (King James' Version).
1616	Captain John Smith writes *A Description of New England*.
1618	Thirty Years' War commences.
	Ralegh beheaded by King James I after being convicted of treason.
1619	The first black slaves are sold in Virginia.
	The first House of Burgesses convenes in Virginia.
1620	The Pilgrim Fathers land in Massachusetts.
1623	Shakespeare's collected plays published.
1625	Charles I is crowned king in England.
	Publication on Hugo Grotius' *De jure belli et pacis*.
1628	King Charles reluctantly accepts the Petition of Right.
1630	The Puritans found Boston, Massachusetts.
	John Winthrop begins his journal, *A History of New England*.
1632	Lord Baltimore founds Maryland.
1635	Maryland's assembly asserts the right to make its own statutes.
	Founding of the Boston Latin School.
1636	Puritans settle Connecticut.
1636	Roger Williams founds Rhode Island.
	Harvard College founded in Massachusetts.
1643	The English Civil War begins.
	Sir Thomas Browne's *Religio Medici* is published.
1644	The Royalists are beaten in the first stage of the Civil War.
	John Milton's *Areopagitica* is published.
1648	Thomas Fuller's book *The Holy State and the Profane State* is published.
1649	Charles I is beheaded.

1650	Jeremy Taylor publishes *The Rule and Exercises of Holy Living*. Cromwell defeats the Royalist Scots; turns back Charles II's first attempt to recover the throne.
1651	Hobbes' *Leviathan* is published.
1653	Cromwell dissolves the Rump Parliament. Settlement of North Carolina begins.
1660	The Protectorate is overthrown; Charles II assumes the English throne.
1664	Settlement of New Jersey begins. Dutch Governor Peter Stuyvesant surrenders New Amsterdam to the English fleet.
1667	John Milton completes *Paradise Lost*.
1669	George Fox organizes the Society of Friends (Quakers). New Amsterdam renamed New York by the English settlers.
1672	Samuel von Pufendorf writes *De jure naturae et gentium*.
1674-1729	Writing of Samuel Sewall's *Diary* (first published 1878-82).
1676	Bacon's Rebellion in Virginia.
1678	John Bunyan's *Pilgrim's Progress* is published.
1679	New Hampshire becomes a royal province.
1680	Settlement of Charleston, South Carolina.
1681	Pennsylvania and Delaware are granted to William Penn. Publication of Part I of John Dryden's *Absalom and Achitophel*.
1682	Penn founds Philadelphia.
1685	James II, a Catholic, succeeds to the throne.
1687	James II publishes the Declaration of Indulgence.
1688	The "Glorious Revolution": William and Mary thrust James from the throne.
1689	The Bill of Rights is accepted by King William and Queen Mary. John Locke's two *Treatises of Civil Government* are published. In North America, King William's War against the French and Indians begins—lasting until 1697.
1690	Locke publishes his *Human Understanding*.
1693	The College of William and Mary is chartered in Virginia.
1701	Yale University founded at New Haven, Connecticut.
1702	Anne, daughter of William and Mary, is crowned queen. In North America, Queen Anne's War begins, lasting until 1713. Publication of *Magnalia Christi Americana*, or *The Ecclesiastical History of New England*, by Cotton Mather.
1711	Joseph Addison begins writing the *Spectator* papers.

1714	George, elector of Hanover, is crowned as George I of the United Kingdom of England and Scotland.
1719	The proprietary administration is overthrown in South Carolina, which becomes a royal province. Daniel Defoe publishes *A Tour through the Whole Island of Great Britain*.
1727	George II succeeds to the throne.
1732	Georgia founded by James Oglethorpe.
1733	Benjamin Franklin begins to publish *Poor Richard's Almanac*.
1735	John Wesley goes out to Georgia, where he preaches until 1738.
1737	George Whitefield goes out to Georgia for a year; he preaches in Massachusetts in 1740.
1740	David Hume publishes *A Treatise of Human Nature*.
1744	King George's War begins, lasting until 1748. Death of William Byrd of Westover, diarist and author of *The History of the Dividing Line Betwixt Virginia and North Carolina* (first published 1841).
1748	College of New Jersey (later Princeton) is founded. Montesquieu publishes *De l'Esprit des Lois*.
1749	Bolingbroke publishes his *Idea of a Patriot King*.
1753	Colonel George Washington resists the French at Fort Necessity.
1754	Benjamin Franklin, at the Albany Congress, proposes a plan of union for the colonies. Jonathan Edwards publishes *The Freedom of the Will*. King's College (later Columbia) is founded in New York. David Hume begins to publish his *History of England*.
1755	The French and Indian War begins, lasting until 1763; Braddock's expedition is defeated. Samuel Johnson publishes *A Dictionary of the English Language*. College of Academy of Philadelphia (later University of Pennsylvania) founded.
1756	Lord Mansfield made chief justice of King's Bench.
1759	Samuel Johnson publishes *Rasselas, Prince of Abyssinia*.
1760	George III is crowned king.
1763	By the Treaty of Paris, France surrenders most of its North American possessions to Britain.
1764	Grenville's Sugar Act vexes the colonies. Brown University founded.

1765 The Stamp Act meets with strong opposition in America.
Lord Rockingham, with Edmund Burke as his private secretary, is reluctantly accepted as prime minister by George III.
William Blackstone begins to publish his *Commentaries on the Laws of England*.

1766 The Rockingham ministry succeeds in repealing the Stamp Act, but passes the Declaratory Act.
Lord Rockingham's government gives way to a ministry dominated by the elder Pitt.
Queen's College (later Rutgers) founded.

1766-
1770 The Townshend Acts rouse furious opposition in America.

1768-
1770 Lord Botetourt serves as governor of Virginia.

1769 Charter of Dartmouth College, New Hampshire.

1770 Lord North's government repeals most of the Townshend duties, but retains a tax upon tea—and stations regiments in Boston.
The Boston "Massacre" (March 5).
Founding of College of Charleston in South Carolina.

1771 Burke appointed London agent for the province of New York.
The Regulators' War in North Carolina.

1773 The Tea Act (May).

1773 The Boston Tea Party (December 16).

1774 The "Intolerable Acts," including the Boston Port Act, passed by Parliament.
The First Continental Congress assembles in Philadelphia.
James Wilson writes a pamphlet declaring the freedom of the colonies from control of Parliament.
Burke's speech at Bristol on the function of a representative (November).

1775 Burke's speech on conciliation (March 22).
The fights at Lexington and Concord (April 9).
The battle of Bunker Hill (June 17).
First publication of John Woolman's *Journals*.
Patrick Henry addresses the Virginia Assembly in Richmond with the demand, "Give me liberty, or give me death" (March 20).

1776 Thomas Paine publishes *Common Sense*.
Jeremy Bentham publishes his *Fragment on Government*.
Adam Smith's *The Wealth of Nations* is published.

The Declaration of Independence (July 4).

Americans defeated in the battle of Brooklyn Heights (August 27).

Edward Gibbon begins to publish his *Decline and Fall of the Roman Empire*.

1777   Burke publishes his *Letter to the Sheriffs of Bristol* (April 30), denouncing the British conduct of the war.

General Burgoyne surrenders to the Americans at Saratoga (October 17).

The Continental Congress draws up the Articles of Confederation.

1778   The United States obtains the alliance of France.

1779   George Rogers Clark gains American victories in the West.

1779-   Jefferson serves as governor of Virginia.
1781

1780   The war is fought chiefly in the South.

Burke declines the poll at Bristol (September 9).

1781   The Articles of Confederation are ratified.

Lord Cornwallis surrenders the British forces at Yorktown.

1782   George III finds it necessary to return the Rockingham Whigs to office, to treat for peace.

1787   John Adams publishes his *Defence of the Constitutions*.

The Constitutional Convention draws up the Constitution of the United States.

1788   Hamilton, Madison, and Jay publish *The Federalist*.

The Constitution is ratified.

1789   George Washington takes office as the first president.

The French Estates-General assemble; the Bastille is stormed.

French Declaration of the Rights of Man and Citizen.

Georgetown University founded.

1790   Burke publishes *Reflections on the Revolution in France*.

1791   John Quincy Adams publishes his *Letters of Publicola*.

The first ten amendments of the Constitution, the "Bill of Rights," are ratified.

1795   Founding of the University of North Carolina.

1796   John Adams elected president.

1798   Publication of William Wordworth's *Lyrical Ballads*, with Samuel Taylor Coleridge.

1799   Publication of *Travels through the State of North America and the Provinces of Upper and Lower Canada during the years 1795, 1796, and 1797*, by Isaac Weld, Jr.

1800   Thomas Jefferson defeats John Adams in the presidential election; beginnings of the "Jeffersonian Revolution."

1801-1824	The "Virginia Dynasty" in national executive power.
1801	John Marshall becomes chief justice of the Supreme Court.
1803	St. George Tucker publishes an American edition of Blackstone's *Commentaries*.
1811	In the House of Representatives, John Randolph speaks against war with England (December 10).
1812	Britain and the United States go to war over shipping and territorial disputes.
1814	Sir Walter Scott publishes his novel *Waverley*.
1815	Andrew Jackson defeats British troops at New Orleans (January 8).
1817	Publication of Coleridge's *Biographia Literaria*. Founding of the University of Michigan.
1819	University of Virginia founded.
1820	Publication of Keats' *Odes*.
1822	Washington Irving publishes *Bracebridge Hall*.
1825	John Quincy Adams inaugurated as president. Beginnings of the "Jacksonian Revolution."
1826	James Kent begins to publish his *Commentaries on American Law*.
1828	Andrew Jackson wins the presidential election. James Fenimore Cooper publishes *Notions of the Americans, Picked up by a Travelling Bachelor*.
1829	Captain Basil Hall publishes *Travels in North America*.
1829-1830	The Virginia Constitutional Convention, which enlarges the franchise.
1831-1832	Tocqueville and Beaumont travel in America.
1832	Publication of Mrs. Trollope's *Domestic Manners of the Americans*.
1833	Joseph Story publishes *Commentaries on the Constitution of the United States*.
1838-1901	Reign of Queen Victoria.
1840	Percy Bysshe Shelley writes *A Defence of Poetry*. Joseph Story publishes *A Familiar Exposition of the Constitution of the United States*.
1844	Charles Dickens publishes *Martin Chuzzlewitt*.
1846	The United States expands to the Pacific.
1850	Dante Gabriel Rosetti publishes *The Blessed Damozel*. John Ruskin publishes *The King of the Golden River*.

1851	John C. Calhoun's *Discourse on the Constitution and Government of the United States* is published.
1857	Anthony Trollope publishes *Barchester Towers*.
1858	William Makepeace Thackeray publishes *The Virginians*.
1859	Edward Fitzgerald publishes his rendering of the *Rubaiyat of Omar Khayyam*. Publication of Alfred Tennyson's *Idylls of the King*.
1860	Abraham Lincoln is elected president.
1861	Sir Henry Maine publishes *Ancient Law*.
1861-1865	The American Civil War.
1863	Nathaniel Hawthorne publishes *Our Old Home*.
1865	Lincoln is assassinated. Birth of William Butler Yeats in Dublin.
1869	Matthew Arnold publishes *Culture and Anarchy*.
1873	Judicature Act, combining English courts of equity and common law.
1875	Birth of Robert Frost in San Francisco.
1876	Opening of Johns Hopkins University in Baltimore.
1880	James Russell Lowell appointed United States minister to the court of St. James.
1883	Publication of Mark Twain's *Life on the Mississippi*. Robert Louis Stevenson publishes *The Silverado Squatters*.
1885	A. V. Dicey publishes *The Law of the Constitution*.
1885-1891	Publication of Henry Adams' *History of the United States during the Administrations of Jefferson and Madison*.
1888	T.S. Eliot born in St. Louis, Missouri.
1889	Birth of Arnold Toynbee in London.
1893	Publication of *The American Commonwealth* by James Bryce.
1901	Barrett Wendell publishes *A Literary History of America*.

Index